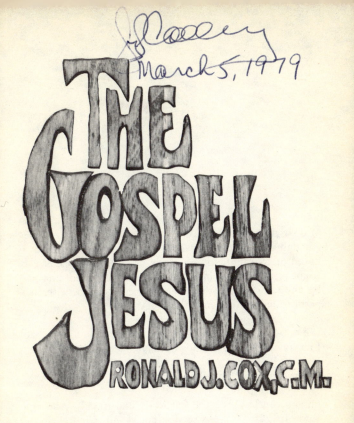

THE GOSPEL JESUS

RONALD J. COX, C.M.

THE STORY IN MODERN ENGLISH

S0-FAE-434

OUR SUNDAY VISITOR, Inc.
NOLL PLAZA, HUNTINGTON, IN 46750

[handwritten] March 5, 1979

ISBN: 0-87973-774-3
Library of Congress Catalog Card Number: 75-43431

Cover Design by James E. McIlrath

Photos courtesy The Catechetical Guild (p. 17), Alinari,
Rome (p. 22), NC News Service (pp. 34 and 165), Religious
News Service (pp. 65, 72, 85, 135, 148 and 153), and Studio
Arte Sacra, Rome (p. 157).

Published, printed and bound in the U.S.A. by
Our Sunday Visitor, Inc.
Noll Plaza
Huntington, Indiana 46750

774

TABLE OF CONTENTS

Preface 7

Part 1 • The God-Man 11

1 / The Angel Gabriel Appears 13
2 / The Great Announcement 15
3 / Mary Goes Visiting.................................... 18
4 / Joseph Marries Mary.................................. 20
5 / The Birth of Jesus 21
6 / Presented to the Lord................................ 24
7 / Homage to a King 25
8 / Working for His Father 27

Part 2 • The Twelve Apostles..................................... 29

9 / Jesus Baptized by John 31
10 / Jesus Tempted by the Devil......................... 33
11 / The First Five Followers 35
12 / First Miracle at a Wedding 37
13 / A Busy Sabbath Day................................. 39
14 / "I Will Make You Fishers of Men".............. 41
15 / Let Down Through the Roof 43
16 / Jesus Calls Matthew 45

17 / "The Sabbath Was Made for Man" 47
18 / The Eight Beatitudes 49
19 / The New Law of Christ 51
20 / Parable of the Good Samaritan 53
21 / The People of God 55
22 / True Inner Holiness 57
23 / Perseverance and Humility 59
24 / A Centurion's Faith in Jesus 61
25 / Parable of the Sower 63
26 / What the Church Is Like 66
27 / A Storm on the Lake 68
28 / A Legion of Devils 69
29 / Miracles for Two Women 71
30 / Jesus Chooses His Twelve 74
31 / Trust in God's Fatherly Care 76
32 / Parable of the Talents 78
33 / The Vine and Its Branches 80
34 / Jesus' Prayer for His Apostles 82
35 / Bread and Fish Multiplied 84
36 / Jesus Walks on the Water 87
37 / Jesus Promises Himself as Food 89
38 / Peter's Profession of Faith 91
39 / A Glimpse of Christ's Glory 93
40 / "One Flock and One Shepherd" 95
41 / Jesus Entrusts His Flock to Peter 97

Part 3 • *Death on a Cross and Victorious Resurrection* 101

42 / Racketeers Driven from the Temple 103
43 / A Cripple at the Pool 106
44 / "Before Abraham Was, I Am" 108
45 / "My Father and I Are One" 110

46 / The Lost Son Comes Back Home 112
47 / Jesus Raises Lazarus from the Dead 114
48 / The King on a Donkey 116
49 / Parable of the Murderous Sharecroppers 118
50 / Jesus Denounces the Hypocrisy of the
        Pharisees 120
51 / Jesus Washes His Apostles' Feet 122
52 / The Last Supper 124
53 / The Way to the Father 126
54 / Jesus Promises the Holy Spirit 128
55 / Why Christians Will Be Hated 130
56 / Jesus' Prayer of Sacrificial Offering 132
57 / Anguish of Mind and Sweat of Blood 134
58 / The Betrayal and Arrest of Jesus 137
59 / Peter Disowns His Master 139
60 / The Jewish Trial 141
61 / The Trial Before the Roman Governor 143
62 / Jesus Flogged, Crowned and Condemned 145
63 / The Crucifixion of Jesus 147
64 / The Death of Jesus 150
65 / The Burial of Jesus 152
66 / The Empty Tomb 155
67 / A Walk to Remember 158
68 / "The Mark of the Nails" 160
69 / A Miraculous Catch of Fish 162
70 / The Ascension of Our Lord 164
71 / The Coming of the Holy Spirit 167
72 / A New Community 169
        Index 170

PREFACE

This book is a digest of the only records we have of the life of Jesus Christ — the Four Gospels. It is a short life of Jesus in a modern version of the Gospels. The material has been reduced to about one-third and concentrates on the primary purpose of Jesus Christ's coming on earth: his becoming man *(Part 1: The God-Man)* in order to extend to all nations *(Part 2: The Twelve Apostles)* the benefits of his atoning death *(Part 3: Death on a Cross and Victorious Resurrection)*.

This short life contains some seventy-two scenes from the Gospels. Presented in a version designed for popular use, they will hopefully bear the same fruits for those who read them as the early Gospel texts bore for their readers.

The Gospel digest is intended primarily for those unfamiliar with the life-story of Jesus. With school-children perhaps it is advisable to have the Gospel selections read aloud. The present version will be found highly suitable for audible reading. This pedagogically wise method will enable the students to grasp more clearly the meaning the original catechesis had for the early Christians. It is helpful to recall that the Gospels were spoken before they were ever written, and that they were written just as they were spoken — in the *Koine* Greek. Reading aloud in this new version will enable one to hear the original Gospels spoken again!

The scriptural citations given at the head of each chapter will enable the reader to locate the sources easily in the Gospels themselves if he wishes to study in their fuller context the selections made. Teachers in particular will find this device helpful. Details of place and time are also given, though these are only of secondary importance (and sometimes conjectural). They are not at all meant to distract from the central figure of the story — Jesus, who is the way, the truth, and the life.

Ronald J. Cox
1911-1970

Eastwood
New South Wales

MAP OF PALESTINE

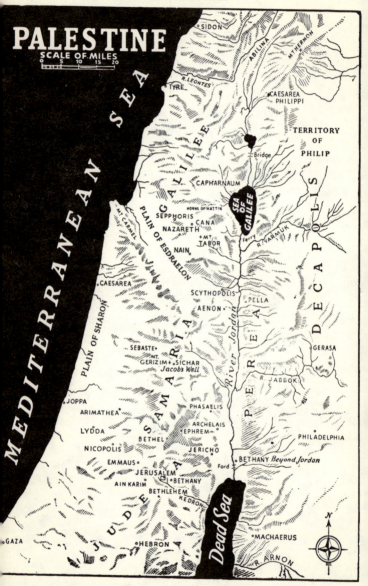

PART 1

The God-Man

Christianity is unique among all religions of the world insofar as its founder, God himself, came down on earth as a mortal man. This historical fact is called "the Incarnation," a Latin word that means "taking flesh." The second of the three persons in God took a human body and soul in the womb of his mother Mary. She remained a virgin because conception took place through the miraculous power of the Holy Spirit (the third person of the Trinity). The name given to the Incarnate Son of God is "Jesus," which means "Savior" in English; the name "Christ" is the Greek for "Messiah," a Hebrew word meaning "the Anointed One" (both priests and kings were anointed with oil). Jesus Christ is usually called "our Lord" in modern speech: it is a title of honor and respect for Jesus as Son of God.

The exact year of our Lord's birth is uncertain. The first B.C.-A.D. calculation, in the sixth century, made an error of at least four years; Jesus must have been born before the death of Herod the Great in

April, 4 B.C. (see Chapter 7). Here December 25, 5 B.C. is accepted as plausible dating (though 6 B.C. would suit just as well). Although not celebrated until the fourth century, December 25 is the traditional birthday of Jesus Christ. The dating of the other events in the chapters of this Part is based on this assumption.

CHAPTER 1

The Angel Gabriel Appears
Luke 1:5-25
The Temple, September, 6 B.C.

When Herod was king of Judea there lived in that country a priest called Zachary and his wife Elizabeth. Both of them were friends of God, but old and childless.

One day, when Zachary was on duty in the Temple, his turn came to go into the Lord's sanctuary and burn incense there, while the rest of the people stood in the courtyard outside, praying.

Suddenly the Lord's angel appeared to the right of the altar of incense. Zachary stood there awestruck, weak with fear.

"There's nothing to be afraid of, Zachary," the angel said. "Your prayer has been heard: your wife will give birth to a son, and you are to name him John. He will be a great joy to you, and his birth will bring much happiness to many people. He is going to be one of God's great men. His work will be to prepare the Jewish race for the Lord's own coming among them; and he will be filled with the Holy Spirit even before he is born."

"How can I be sure of this?" Zachary asked the angel. "I'm an old man now, and my wife's on in years, too."

The angel replied: "I have come direct from the Lord himself; Gabriel is my name. The good news

I've just brought you is the Lord's own message; but since you don't believe it, as a punishment you will not be able to speak a word until your son is born."

While this was going on, the people were waiting for Zachary and wondering why he was so long in the sanctuary. When at last he did appear he could only make signs to them; no matter how hard he tried, not a single word came from his lips.

When his term of duty ended he went home, and soon his wife became pregnant. "The Lord has taken pity on me," she said; "no one can despise me anymore."

CHAPTER 2

The Great Announcement
Luke 1:26-38

Nazareth, March 25, 5 B.C.

Just six months later God sent the angel Gabriel to a Galilean town called Nazareth with a message to a virgin engaged to Joseph, of David's royal blood; her name was Mary.

The angel entered her home and said: "Rejoice, joyful Lady of Grace; the Lord is with you."

She was deeply moved by these words and wondered what the greeting meant.

So the angel spoke again: "There's no need to be afraid, Mary; no one is dearer to the heart of God. You are to become a mother; Jesus is the name you shall give your son. He is destined for greatness; men will call him Son of the Most High. The Lord God will give him the throne of his father David, and he shall rule over Jacob's household forever — his kingdom shall never have an end."

Mary replied to the angel: *"How* can this come about? I have vowed myself to a life of virginity."

And he answered: "The Holy Spirit will come down upon you, and the Most High will cast the power of his shadow* over you; that's why this holy

---

*A reference to the *shekinah,* the bright, luminous cloud of God's presence during the exodus from Egypt, in the thirteenth century B.C.

child of yours shall be known as God's own son.

"Didn't everyone think your relative Elizabeth incapable of bearing children? Well, she is six months pregnant. There is nothing God cannot do."

Then Mary said: "I surrender myself completely to the Lord; let him possess me just as you have said."

And with that the angel left her.

THE ANNUNCIATION

CHAPTER 3

Mary Goes Visiting
Luke 1:39-77
Ain Karim, April-June, 5 B.C.

Without delay Mary got ready and hurried off to a town in the Judean hills, where Zachary lived. She went straight to his house and called out to Elizabeth. At the sound of Mary's voice Elizabeth's unborn baby jumped for joy, and she was moved by the Holy Spirit to proclaim in ringing tones: "You are the most blessed of all women, and your child is highest in God's favor, too. What an honor to have the Savior's own mother pay me a visit!"

Then Mary said: "How good the Lord is! My heart and soul are brimming over with joy, because God my Savior has smiled so lovingly on poor, unworthy me. Truly, from now on the whole world will call me the happiest woman that ever lived: the Almighty himself (blessed be his holy name!) has done such wonderful things to me."

Mary stayed with Elizabeth for three months, until Elizabeth's child was born. Eight days later relatives and friends gathered at the house for the circumcision ceremony; they were thinking of calling him Zachary, after his father. But his mother wouldn't hear of it. "No," she said, "he's to be called John."

So they appealed to his father (secretly so that Elizabeth wouldn't know of it). What name did *he* want? Zachary wrote: "His name is John."

And at that moment his speech was restored. Inspired by the Holy Spirit he spoke these prophetic words: "Blessed be the Lord God of Israel! At last he has begun the plan of salvation for his people by raising up a mighty savior of David's royal blood. He will come to us like the rising sun, bringing light to those who live in darkness and death's shadow, guiding our steps along the road that leads to peace.

"And you, our own little boy, you will march ahead of the Lord to clear the road for him, alerting his people to that salvation which alone can bring them forgiveness of their sins."

CHAPTER 4

Joseph Marries Mary

Matthew 1:18-24

Nazareth, July, 5 B.C.

At this time Mary and Joseph were only engaged; they hadn't yet begun to live together.*

When Joseph was told she was with child, he made up his mind to break off the engagement quietly; being a considerate man he didn't wish to submit her to the humiliation of a public court case.

While he was thinking over this decision, the Lord's angel appeared to him in a dream. "Joseph, son of David," he said, "don't be afraid to take Mary into your home as your wife. Even though her child has been conceived by the power of the Holy Spirit, *you* are the one chosen to name him Jesus; he is the Savior of a sinful race."

All this took place so that the Lord's prophecy might come true: "See, the virgin shall be with child, and the son she bears will be truly Emmanuel†."

When Joseph woke up he remembered what the angel had told him to do. So he went and brought Mary into his home as his bride.

*Joseph was about twenty years old at this time. An early apocryphal book wrongly made him an old man to explain Jesus' "brethren" as children of Joseph by a previous marriage. They were really his cousins.

†"God-with-us": an allusion to the coming of God into the world in human form. It also signifies "God-our-helper," which means "savior."

20

Chapter 5

The Birth of Jesus
Luke 2:1-20
Bethlehem, December 25, 5 B.C.

This was the year of the emperor Augustus' decree ordering a census of the whole world.

Everyone had to go to his home to register; so Joseph traveled from Nazareth to Bethlehem, the ancestral home of King David's clan. Mary went along with him, too; and during their stay her confinement came. She gave birth to a son (her firstborn), dressed him in his baby clothes, and laid him to sleep in a feedbox, for there was no room for them in the house overhead.*

That same night shepherds were guarding their sheep nearby, when the Lord's angel appeared among them; a bright light bathed everything in divine glory. "Don't be frightened," the angel said. "I bring good news: this very day a savior has been born, here in David's own town; he is the Lord Messiah in person.

"How will you find him? Look for a baby in an animal's feedbox."

And all at once thousands of angels were there

---

*It is felt that the commonly interpreted "inn" is better rendered as "the house overhead." The same Greek word, *kataluma,* is "the upstairs room" of the Last Supper (see Chapter 52); whereas "the inn" of the Good Samaritan, for instance (see Chapter 20), is a different Greek word altogether, *pandocheion.*

singing God's praises: "Glory be to God in heaven above, and peace on earth to men through his saving love."

As soon as the angels left, the shepherds hurried off to Bethlehem, where they found Mary and Joseph — *and* the baby lying in a feedbox. They made known all they had been told about the child, and then went back to their sheep.

But Mary treasured up all these memories and thought about them over and over again.

Note: For the account of the circumcision and naming of Jesus, see Luke 2:21.

(FACING PAGE)
THE BIRTH OF JESUS

CHAPTER 6

Presented to the Lord
Luke 2:22-38
The Temple, February 2, 4 B.C.

All Jewish firstborn sons belonged to the Lord, and the Mosaic Law demanded that they be bought back for a pair of doves. So when the time came, Jesus' parents took him up to Jerusalem to present him to the Lord.

In Jerusalem at the time there was a good, devout man called Simeon; the Holy Spirit had told him he would live to see the Messiah in person. He came into the Temple (guided by the Holy Spirit) just when the child Jesus was brought there by his parents; and he, too, was privileged to hold the child in his arms.

He spoke this hymn of praise to God: "Now, Master, you can let your servant go in peace. I have seen the Savior of the world with my own eyes: a light to the pagans and the glory of the Jewish race."

While his father and mother were still filled with wonder at these words, Simeon blessed them and said to Mary: "This child shall make or break men . . . they will either accept or reject him. And you will suffer with him — a sword thrust through your heart!"

At that moment Anna joined them, and began to praise God out loud. She was a very old widow who spent all her time in the Temple continually praying and fasting. From this day on she never stopped talking about the child to all who longed for freedom.

CHAPTER 7

Homage to a King
Matthew 2:1-23
Bethlehem, February, 4 B.C.

While Herod still ruled in Judea, a group of wise men from the East arrived in Jerusalem, asking: "Where is the newborn king of the Jews? We saw his star rise and have come to bow down before him."

When King Herod heard this news he felt uneasy. He sent for his learned men and inquired where the Messiah was to be born. They quoted him the Scripture passage: "You are not really such an insignificant town, Bethlehem; from you a leader will rise up to be the shepherd of Israel."

Then Herod had a private audience with the three astrologers and questioned them about the exact time the star had appeared. Satisfied, he directed them to Bethlehem: "Go and find the child, and then let me know the place so that I, too, can come down and worship him."

Off they went; and there was the star again leading them on until it stopped right above the place where the child was. Filled with an indescribable joy, they entered the house to find the child there with his mother Mary. They dropped to their knees in adoration and opening up their treasure chests they offered him their presents: gold, incense and myrrh.

They didn't go back to Herod, but (under divine command) returned home unobserved. No sooner had they gone than the Lord's angel woke Joseph in the middle of the night: "Be quick now! Take the child and his mother with you into Egypt. Herod will soon be searching for the child to kill him."

When Herod found out the wise men had fooled him, he was furious. He sent his soldiers into Bethlehem with orders to kill every boy under two years of age.

As soon as Herod was dead, the angel appeared again to Joseph telling him it was safe to return. And so he came to live in Nazareth — their own town. There the child grew up, big and strong; he was quick to learn, and a holy boy, too.

Chapter 8

Working for His Father
Luke 2:41-52
The Temple, April, 9 A.D.

Every year his parents went up to Jerusalem for the Passover. When he was twelve they took him along with them. After the paschal ceremonies they set off back home; but Jesus stayed behind in Jerusalem. His parents did not know this (they thought he was with others in the party) until the end of the day. They inquired then and found he was missing; so they turned back toward Jerusalem, searching for him.

They did not find him until the third day. There he was, in the Temple among the teachers, taking part in their learned discussions. Around them a crowd had gathered, thrilled at his brilliant answers.

This scene filled his parents with deep emotion. "My dear son," his mother said to him, "why have you done this to us? Your father and I have been frantic with worry, looking everywhere for you."

He replied: "Why have you been searching for me? Where could I be but at work in my Father's house?"

They did not fully grasp what he meant. But he went back to Nazareth with them, and lived there ever obedient and submissive to them. And all the time his mother treasured up in her heart every little happening, while Jesus grew in body and mind, a favorite with God and men.

MAP OF GALILEE

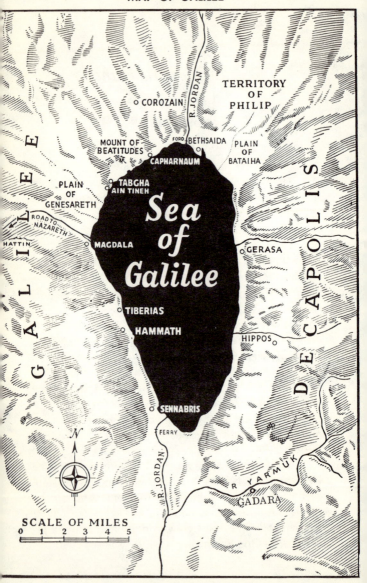

COROZAIN

R. JORDAN

TERRITORY
OF
PHILIP

FORD BETHSAIDA

MOUNT OF
BEATITUDES

PLAIN
OF
BATAIHA

CAPHARNAUM

PLAIN
OF
GENESARETH

TABGHA
AIN TINEH

Sea
of
Galilee

ROAD TO
NAZARETH

HATTIN

MAGDALA

GERASA

DECAPOLIS

GALILEE

TIBERIAS

HAMMATH

HIPPOS

SENNABRIS

N

FERRY

R. JORDAN

R. YARMUK

GADARA

SCALE OF MILES
0 1 2 3 4 5

PART 2

The Twelve Apostles

Sunk 600 feet below sea level in a basin of bare, brown hills is a brilliant blue lake in the north of Palestine. From its shape it got the name of Genesareth — "the harp." But it is commonly known as the Lake or Sea of Galilee.

Although only a tiny lake in size (about thirteen by seven miles), it is surely the most sacred body of water in the world: by its shores our Lord spent the greater part of his public life. He settled at Capharnaum on the northwest shore in the spring (May) of 28 A.D. and never left the lakeside for any length of time for the next sixteen months — until late summer (September) of 29 A.D. Almost all of the thirty-three scenes in this Part are located by the lakeside.

The lake was the very heart of Galilee. It was not an out-of-the-way place like Nazareth. It had a population of 100,000 settled around it and was on the main trade routes of the East. Greeks and Romans rubbed shoulders with the native Jews. It was indeed a most suitable place for our Lord to lay the foundations of his kingdom, which was to include all peoples.

This was Jesus' primary mission by the lakeside. Although crowds of people witnessed the many miracles that took place there, the apostles are the key characters in the story. The last twelve chapters of this Part (Chapters 30 to 41) are devoted to apostolic training. Our Lord selects twelve of his followers to be his apostles. They spend most of their time together and travel about in close daily intimacy with the Master.

He trains them to a new outlook, to see things as he sees them himself. He teaches them how to understand and tell others the good news of salvation (the Gospel). They are the men whom he destines to bring the fruits of his atoning death to the whole world, through membership in his kingdom.

The climax of this stage of our Lord's life comes at the foot of Mount Hermon, a mountain towering 9,000 feet to the north of the lake. There Peter makes his profession of faith in the divinity of Jesus (Chapter 38): the long, gradual training of the Twelve has been brought to a successful conclusion.

Chapter 9

Jesus Baptized by John
Luke 3:1-8, 21-22; Matthew 3:1-17;
Mark 1:1-11; John 1:30-34

Jordan River, January, 28 A.D.

In the fifteenth year of the emperor Tiberius' reign, when Pontius Pilate was governor of Judea, and Herod prince in Galilee during the high priest-hood of Annas and Caiphas, a message came from God through John: "The kingdom of God has come at last; you must be converted from your sinful ways."

And he went up and down the Jordan valley preaching to great crowds of Jews who confessed their sins while he baptized them in the Jordan river.

When he noticed Pharisees and Sadducees among those waiting for baptism he said: "Who warned you, poisonous reptiles, to escape from the divine punishment that is coming? Don't deceive yourselves that descent from Abraham makes you in-dispensable to God. Why, he can raise up children [*banim*] to Abraham from these very stones [*aba-nim*]!"

At this time Jesus came from Nazareth and pre-sented himself to John for baptism. But John tried to stop him: "I'm the one that ought to be baptized by you; *you* shouldn't be coming to me."

Jesus said: "Go ahead and do as I ask; this is how we are to carry out every detail of the divine plan."

31

So John gave way and baptized him. When Jesus came out of the water he stood on the bank lost in prayer. Suddenly the clouds were torn apart and the Holy Spirit came down upon him in bodily form, like a dove. A voice rang out loud and clear: "You are my dearly loved son; I am well pleased with you."

When some Pharisees asked John if he were the Messiah, he said: "Remember I told you there was a man right here among you whose sandal strap I was not worthy to untie; although he came after me in time, he existed before I was born. Well, I myself did not know who he was until God gave me this clue, 'You will see the Spirit coming down from heaven like a dove and resting on him; he is the One who is to baptize with the Holy Spirit.'

"Yes, I saw this happen and can now tell you truly: This person is the Son of God."

Chapter 10

Jesus Tempted by the Devil

Luke 4:1-13; Matthew 4:1-11; Mark 1:12-13

Judean Desert, January-February, 28 A.D.

Impelled by the Holy Spirit Jesus turned away from the Jordan and climbed up into the barren hills nearby to be put to the test by the devil. For forty days and nights he lived with wild beasts and during all that time he ate nothing at all; at the end of it he was very hungry.

Then the tempter came near and said to him: "If you really are God's son, order these stones to turn into loaves of bread."

He answered: "Scripture says, 'Man cannot live by bread alone; life is to be found in every word that comes from the mouth of God.' "

Next the devil accompanied Jesus into Jerusalem and there dared him to stand on the highest corner of the Temple courtyard, saying to him: "If you really *are* God's son, jump down from here; Scripture says, 'He shall give his angels charge over you to keep you safe, and they will hold you up with their hands so that you may not hurt your foot against a stone.' "

Jesus replied: "On the other hand, Scripture says, 'You shall not put the Lord your God on trial.' "

Finally, the devil led him up to the top of a very

THE CITY OF JERUSALEM

high mountain, from which he showed him all the kingdoms of the world in a single vision: "I will give you command over all these and the glory that belongs to them. Come then, all shall be yours if you will go down on your knees in adoration — just once!"

Then Jesus said to him: "Away with you, Satan! Scripture says, 'You shall worship the Lord your God and serve none but him.' "

So the devil withdrew, biding his time; and immediately angels appeared, bringing food for Jesus to eat.

CHAPTER 11

The First Five Followers
John 1:35-51
Bethany Beyond Jordan, March, 28 A.D.

John was still by the Jordan with two of his followers. Unable to take his eyes off Jesus walking by, he said: "Look, there he is! The Lamb of God who is to take away the world's sins." The two disciples heard him say it, and followed Jesus.

When he noticed them Jesus turned and asked: "Is there something I can do for you?"

"Yes, Master; where do you live?"

"Why don't you come and see?"

So they went and saw where he was staying. They were his guests all the rest of the day — from about four o'clock in the afternoon. One of the two was Andrew, Simon Peter's brother.* Early next morning he went in search of his brother to tell him: "We have found the Messiah!" And he brought him to Jesus.

Jesus looked into his heart and said: "So your name is Simon, son of John; well, you shall be called Kepha†."

---

*Andrew's companion was John.

†An Aramaic word — the language spoken by Jesus. In Greek — the language of the Gospels — it is *Petros,* which means *Rock* in English. In the ancient East, to give a new name to a person indicated ownership: Peter now belongs to Jesus (see Chapter 38).

Next day Jesus decided to set out for Galilee. He met Philip and said to him: "Follow me." Then Philip told Nathanael*: "We have found the man spoken of by Moses and the prophets; he is Jesus of Nazareth, son of Joseph."

"From Nazareth!" Nathanael objected. "Can anything good come from that place?"

"Come and see for yourself," replied Philip.

When Jesus saw Nathanael coming he said: "Now here's a real Israelite, tried and true."

"How can you possibly know anything about me?"

"I saw you under the fig tree — before Philip called you."

"Master, you are the Son of God! You are the King of Israel!"

"What! You believe simply because I told you that I saw you under the fig tree? I solemnly assure you that you will experience much greater things than this. Why, even heaven itself shall be wide open to the gaze of everyone of you, with God's angels going up and coming down upon the Son of Man unceasingly."

*"Bartholomew" in the list of the Twelve.

CHAPTER 12

First Miracle at a Wedding
John 2:1-11
Cana in Galilee, March, 28 A.D.

Two days later there was a wedding at Cana in Galilee, at which Jesus' mother was present. Jesus and his followers were also guests.

When the supply of wine ran out, Jesus' mother said to him: "They're out of wine."

He answered her: "Are you asking me, O Woman of Destiny,* to anticipate the hour set down by my Father?"

His mother said to the servants: "Be sure to do whatever he tells you."

Now, the Jews always wash their hands before meals, and for this purpose six twenty-gallon jars were standing there on the floor. When Jesus told them to fill the jars with water, they filled them right to the brim.

Then he said to them: "Now draw some out and give a cupful to the master of ceremonies."

So they brought it to him, and he tasted this water — which had now been turned into wine. He had no idea where it came from; only the servants who had drawn the water knew that.

He called the bridegroom and said to him: "Everyone I know serves the best wine first, and the

*Simply "Woman" in the original — a term of honor (see Chapter 63).

poorer kind only when the guests have had plenty to
drink; but you have kept the best wine until the last!"

So, in Cana of Galilee, Jesus worked his first
miracle: a sign that made known the glorious power
he possessed. By it the growing faith of his followers
in him was deepened.

CHAPTER 13

A Busy Sabbath Day
Matthew 4:12-16; 8:14-17;
Luke 4:31-43

Capharnaum, May, 28 A.D.

And now Jesus came and settled down in Capharnaum, a lakeside town. In this way the prophecy of Isaiah came true: "People living in darkness have seen a great light; light has dawned upon men living in a land overshadowed by death."

He began teaching there on the sabbath day. Everyone was thrilled at his teaching: he spoke with authority, quite unlike the doctors of the law. A possessed man in the synagogue there began shouting at the top of his voice: "Hey you! What are you interfering for, Jesus of Nazareth? Have you come to destroy us? I know who you are: God's Holy One."

Jesus sharply rebuked the evil spirit: "Hold your tongue! Go out of him!" Then it threw the man into a convulsion before the eyes of the onlookers and with a shriek came out without hurting him in the slightest. A sense of awe fell upon all as they talked the matter over: "See his power over the evil spirits; a word of command and out they come!"

He went straight from the synagogue to Simon's mother-in-law who was ill in bed with a severe fever. He took her by the hand and the fever left her. She got up right away and insisted on serving them a meal.

When it was evening and the sun had set, the

people kept on bringing him all who were sick or possessed by devils, so that the whole town stood crowding there at the door. He placed his hands on each in turn and healed them all.

Before daybreak he got up and went away to a quiet place to pray. Simon and his companions went to look for him. When they found him they said: "Everybody is asking for you."

He replied: "But we must go to other towns as well, to tell them the good news of the kingdom of God; that is the reason I left home."

CHAPTER 14

"I Will Make You Fishers of Men"

Luke 5:1-11; Matthew 4:18-22;
Mark 1:16-20

Lake of Galilee, May, 28 A.D.

While Jesus was walking by the lake of Genesareth one day, the crowds were pressing close about
to hear the word of God. Two boats were drawn up
on the beach — the fishermen had gone ashore to
clean their nets. He went on board one of the boats,
which belonged to Simon, and asked him to row out
a little way from the shore; he then sat down and
began to teach the crowds from the boat.

When he stopped speaking he said to Simon:
"Take her out into deep water and let down your net
for a catch."

Simon answered: "Master, we've worked hard
all night and haven't caught a thing, but if you say so
I'll let down the net."

They did so and netted such a huge shoal of fish
that the net was near breaking; so they made signals
to their partners in the other boat to come and help
them. They filled both boats to sinking point.

On seeing this, Simon Peter threw himself down
at Jesus' feet: "No, Lord, please not *me*; I'm just a
plain sinner."

But Jesus said to him: "There's nothing to be
afraid of; from now on your catch will be *men*."

When they beached their boats Jesus called Simon and his brother Andrew: "Come, follow me; I will make you fishers of men." There and then they dropped their nets and became his followers.

Then he went a little farther along the shore and called the two brothers James and John; at once they left their father Zebedee in the boat with his crew and followed Jesus.

CHAPTER 15

Let Down Through the Roof
Matthew 9:1-8; Mark 2:1-12;
Luke 5:17-26

Capharnaum, June, 28 A.D.

One day Jesus returned to his hometown, Capharnaum. As soon as the news spread that he was back, such a crowd gathered that there was no room left even about the doorway. Among his audience were Pharisees and doctors of the law from all Galilee and Judea — even from Jerusalem itself.

While he was preaching, four men arrived carrying a paralyzed man on a stretcher; they intended to bring him in and put him down at Jesus' feet. When they found it impossible to get near him because of the dense crowd, they went up on top of the house, stripped the tiles from the roof over Jesus' head, and let the man down, stretcher and all, through the hole, right in front of Jesus.

Seeing their faith he said to the paralytic: "Have confidence, my son; your sins are here and now forgiven."

At this some of the lawyers and Pharisees thought to themselves: "That's blasphemy! What right has this man to talk like that? No one can forgive sins but God — *and God alone.*"

But Jesus read their minds and said straight out: "I know what you are thinking: it's easy enough to make such a claim, but a different matter to *prove* it.

43

So I will now demonstrate to you that the Son of Man has power on earth to forgive sins."

Then he spoke to the paralyzed man: "Stand up! Take your bed with you and go home."

Instantly he sprang to his feet before their eyes, picked up his stretcher, and walked away, blessing God as he went.

Sheer amazement gripped every man present, as in awed voices they praised God for giving such powers to men*: "We never saw anything like this before; we've seen incredible things today."

*Note the plural, an allusion to the same power of forgiving sins to be given later by Jesus to the apostles (see Chapter 41).

CHAPTER 16

Jesus Calls Matthew
Matthew 9:9-17; Mark 2:13-22;
Luke 5:27-39

Tabgha Wharf, June, 28 A.D.

After this he went out by the lakeside; all the people came out to him and he taught them there.

Then as he walked farther on he noticed a tax collector called Matthew, son of Cleophas, sitting at work in the customs house. He said to him: "Follow me."

There and then he got up from his table, quit his business, and followed Jesus.

Later on, Matthew gave a dinner for him at his own house. At table with Jesus and his disciples there was a large number of tax collectors and sinners. When the lawyers and Pharisees saw him taking a meal in such bad company, they complained to his disciples: "Why does your master eat and drink with tax collectors and sinners?"

Jesus heard it and said: "Healthy people don't need a doctor, but the sick do. It is my mission to call sinners, not saints, to reform their lives."

At this time John the Baptist's disciples were keeping a fast day; they came to Jesus with the question: "Why do your followers eat and drink while we fast — and the Pharisees, too?"

He replied: "Surely, you don't expect wedding guests to be sad while the bridegroom is with them?

But the day will come when he will be taken away from them; that will be the time for fasting."

And he gave them these illustrations: "Nobody cuts a piece from a new coat to patch an old one; if he does, he will ruin the new coat, and the piece, being unshrunk, will tear away from the old coat, and a worse tear is made. Nor does anybody pour new wine into old wineskins; if he does, the new wine will burst the skins, the wine will be spilled, and the skins will be ruined. No, new wine must go into new wineskins, and so both are saved."

CHAPTER 17

"The Sabbath Was Made for Man"

Matthew 12:1-21;
Mark 2:23-28; 3:1-6; Luke 6:1-11

Capharnaum, June, 28 A.D.

It happened that Jesus was walking through the wheatfields on the sabbath day; and as his followers were hungry they began picking the ears of wheat and eating them, rubbing them between their hands. The Pharisees, seeing it, said to him: "Look at that! Why are they doing what is not allowed on the sabbath?"

So he spoke to them: "Have you never read how David went into God's House and ate the sacred loaves (reserved by law for the priests) when he was hungry — and gave them to his companions as well? Or again have you not read in the law that the priests can break the sabbath rest in the Temple and nobody blames them? The sabbath was made for man, not man for the sabbath. It follows that the Son of Man is master even of the sabbath."

On another sabbath day he went into the synagogue to teach; and a man with a withered hand stood there. "Is it right to heal anyone on the sabbath day?" the lawyers and Pharisees asked, hoping to bring a charge against him.

He knew what was going on in their minds; so he said to the man with the shriveled hand: "Stand up and come out here in front."

Then he addressed them: "If one of your sheep fell into a pit on the sabbath day, wouldn't you pull it out? Surely a *man* is more important than a sheep! It is clear then there is nothing wrong in doing a work of mercy on the sabbath."

They sat there in dead silence as he looked around at them in anger, grieved at the hardness of their hearts. Then he spoke to the man: "Stretch out your hand!" He did so and it became as sound as the other one.

The Pharisees, filled with insane fury, walked out of the synagogue and at once began plotting how to put him to death.

Jesus was aware of this and withdrew with his followers from that place. Great crowds followed him, bringing their sick and those possessed by evil spirits; he healed all their diseases and drove out the devils. In this way the prophecy of Isaiah came true: "Here is my Chosen One; I am well pleased with him. He will not snap the crushed reed or snuff out the smoldering wick."

CHAPTER 18

The Eight Beatitudes
Matthew 4:23 — 5:16; Mark 3:7-12;
Luke 6:17-26

Mount of Beatitudes, June, 28 A.D.

Jesus traveled all over Galilee, teaching in the synagogues the good news of the kingdom. They brought to him all the sick and suffering, and he healed them.

Such vast crowds followed him that he went up onto the hillside and sat down with his followers around him. This is what he said to them:

"Truly happy are the humble; the kingdom is already theirs.

"Truly happy are the gentle; the promised land shall be their possession.

"Truly happy are the sorrowful; they shall be consoled.

"Truly happy are those who hunger and thirst for holiness; they shall be completely satisfied.

"Truly happy are the compassionate; God will be compassionate to them.

"Truly happy are those with a clear conscience; they shall see God.

"Truly happy are those who love and spread peace; God will call them his sons.

"Truly happy are those who bear the marks of torture for the truth; the kingdom is already theirs.

"What happiness will be yours when people

blame you, persecute you, and tell lies about you because of me! Be glad then; yes, jump for joy, because a rich reward awaits you in heaven.

"You are the salt of the earth; you are the light of the world. People do not light a lamp and put it away under a box; no, they put it on a stand where it gives light to everyone in the house. Your light must shine like that before your fellowmen so that they can see the good you do and give glory to your Father in heaven."

CHAPTER 19

The New Law of Christ
Matthew 5:17-48; Luke 6:27-36
Mount of Beatitudes, June, 28 A.D.

"My mission is to bring the law to its true perfection — every dot and comma of it. It is not my purpose to abolish or destroy the law.

"This commandment is well known to you all: 'You shall not murder; if a man commits murder, he must answer for it before the court of justice.' But I go farther and tell you that any man who gets angry with his brother or insults him must answer for it in hellfire. So if you are offering your gift at the altar, and there recall that your brother has a grievance against you, leave your gift before the altar, and first be reconciled to your brother, and then come and offer your gift.

"You know this commandment, too: 'You shall not commit adultery.' But I go farther and tell you that he who looks at a woman with desire has already committed adultery with her in his heart. Yes, if your right eye makes you fall into sin, pluck it out and throw it away; better to lose one part of your body than to have the whole cast into hell.

"This is another prescription: 'An eye for an eye and a tooth for a tooth.' But I on the contrary am telling you not to meet evil with evil. If a man hits you on the right cheek, turn the other cheek to him as well; if anyone takes your coat, let him have your shirt with it. Treat other people exactly as you would have them treat you. That sums up the whole law.

"You have heard the saying: 'Love your neighbor, but not your enemy.' My teaching is: Love your enemies, pray for your persecutors, and then you will be true sons of your heavenly Father who makes his sun rise on the good and bad alike, who makes his rain fall on sinners as well as on saints. If you love only your friends, what's praiseworthy in that? Even worldly men do as much. If you greet only your neighbors, what's wonderful in that? Why, even the pagans do as much. No, it's your *enemies* you must love, and do acts of kindness to them without expecting to get anything back. You must have the perfect charity of your heavenly Father: all goodness and kindness to ungrateful and evil men."

CHAPTER 20

Parable of the Good Samaritan
Luke 10:25-37
Bethany, November, 29 A.D.

It happened once that an expert in the law came forward to put a searching question to Jesus: "Master, what must I do to make sure of eternal life?"

Jesus asked him: "What does the law say about it?"

He answered: "Love the Lord your God with the love of your whole heart and soul, with all the strength and power of your whole being; and love your neighbor as yourself."

"That's right," Jesus said to him; "do this and you shall find life."

But he, eager to justify his question, asked: "But who is my neighbor?"

And Jesus gave him his answer: "Once upon a time a man was on his way down from Jerusalem to Jericho where he fell into the hands of robbers, who stripped him of his clothes, beat him up, and went off leaving him half dead.

"Now it happened that a priest was going along the same road; he saw him there and went around the other side of the hill. So, too, did a Levite who came to that place; he took a look at him and then turned away.

"But a Samaritan traveler was filled with compassion the moment he saw him; he went up and bandaged his wounds, bathing them first with wine and oil. Then he put him on his own donkey and brought him to the inn, where he cared for him. In the morning he gave the innkeeper two days' pay: 'Look after him, will you? If there are any further expenses, I guarantee payment on my way back.'

"Which of these three, do you think, proved himself a true neighbor to the robbers' victim?"

"The one that helped him," he replied.

Then Jesus said: "Go and do as he did."

CHAPTER 21

The People of God
Matthew 25:31-46
Bethany, April, 30 A.D.

Another day Jesus said: "When the Son of Man comes back in glory, all nations will be summoned before his throne. He will divide them into two groups (just as a shepherd does): the sheep on his right, the goats on his left.

"Then the king will say to those on his right: 'Come into the eternal kingdom; you belong to the Father's household now. . . . Once I was hungry and thirsty and you gave me food and drink; I was homeless and you made me welcome, in rags and you clothed me, ill and you looked after me, a prisoner and you came to visit me.'

"Then the good will reply: 'Lord, when did we see you hungry and thirsty and give you food and drink? When did we see you homeless and bring you to our home, in rags and clothe you, ill or in prison and come to visit you?'

"And the king will answer: 'Truly, when you did it to the most insignificant follower of mine, you did it to me.'

"Then he will say to those on his left: 'Go far from my presence into everlasting fire with the devil and his angels. . . . Once I was hungry and thirsty, but you gave me nothing to eat or drink; I was homeless and you turned me away, in rags and you did not clothe me, ill and in prison but you ignored me.'

"Then they, too, will reply: 'Lord, when did we ever see you hungry or thirsty, homeless or in rags, ill or in prison and failed to come to your aid?'

"And he will answer: 'Truly, when you refused help to even the most insignificant follower of mine, you refused it to me.'

"And so they shall go their separate ways: these to eternal punishment, but the good to eternal life."

CHAPTER 22

True Inner Holiness
Matthew 6:1-18; 7:24-27;
Luke 11:1-4; 6:47-49

Mount of Beatitudes, June, 28 A.D.

"Be careful not to make a display of your religion in public just to attract notice; if you do, there's no place for you in your heavenly Father's house.

"When you do an act of charity don't tell the whole world about it. Only hypocrites look for the esteem and applause of men; believe me, that is all the reward they will get. No, you must do your good deeds secretly, not letting your left hand know what your right hand is doing; and then your Father, who knows all secrets, will reward you.

"When you pray don't be like those hypocrites who must have an audience; they stand at street corners so everyone can see them. Believe me, that is all they will get. No, you must go into a room by yourself, shut the door, and pray to your Father in secret; and then your Father, who knows all secrets, will reward you.

"Don't imitate the pagans who imagine that the more they talk, the more likely their prayers will be heard. You don't have to say much; your heavenly Father knows well what your needs are before you ask him. This is how to pray:

" 'Our heavenly Father, may your name be honored;

May your kingdom come and your will be done
on earth as it is in heaven.
Please give us day after day the food we need.
Forgive us our sins as we have already forgiven
those
who have offended us.
Keep us clear of temptation and protect us from
all evil.'

"When you fast don't draw attention to the fact
by going about with a gloomy face; that is sheer hypocrisy. You should look bright and gay, so that nobody can tell you are fasting; and then your Father,
who knows all secrets, will reward you.

"You must not only listen to my words; you
must put them into practice. If you do so, you are like
the wise man who built his house on rock; the rain
fell, the floods rose, the winds blew and beat upon
that house — but it did not fall. If you don't act upon
my words, you are like the foolish man who built on
sand; the rain fell, the floods rose, the winds blew —
and down crashed that house in ruins."

CHAPTER 23

Perseverance and Humility
Matthew 7:7-8; Luke 11:9-10; 18:1-14
Jordan Valley, February, 30 A.D.

Another time Jesus told a story encouraging his followers to persevere in prayer and never give up: "In a certain town there lived a judge who was not afraid of anyone — God or man. Now, there was a widow in this town who kept coming to him and demanding damages in a lawsuit.

"For a time he refused, but later thought it over: 'Although I'm not afraid of anybody, yet this woman is such a nuisance I will push her case through before she drives me mad.' "

Then Jesus concluded: "Those are the words of an *unjust* judge. And do you think God will turn a deaf ear when his friends are appealing to him day and night? Of course not; he will quickly come to their aid.

"So take the lesson to heart: Ask and ask again, and you will get your request; keep on searching and you will find the treasure; keep on knocking and the door will open for sure."

Then he told another story about those who were convinced of their own goodness and looked down on everyone else: "Two men went to pray in the Temple — a Pharisee and a tax collector. The Pharisee stood upright, head held high, and said this prayer: 'I thank you, O God, that I'm not like the rest

59

of men, all thieves, liars, adulterers — like that tax collector over there. I fast twice a week and pay a tax of ten percent on every item of my income.'

"But the tax collector remained in the background, bowed down, beating his breast and saying: 'O God, have mercy on me — a sinner.'

"I assure you, this man went back home high in God's favor; but not the other. Because everyone who thinks highly of himself will be humbled, but anyone who humbles himself will be raised to great heights."

Chapter 24

A Centurion's Faith in Jesus
Luke 7:1-10; Matthew 8:11-13
Capharnaum, June, 28 A.D.

A centurion who lived in Capharnaum had a highly esteemed servant lying paralyzed in bed at his house; he was in great pain and at the point of death.

The centurion had heard about Jesus. So he sent some Jewish elders asking him to come and save his servant's life.

These men presented themselves before Jesus, earnestly pleading with him: "He deserves this favor from you; he is a good friend to our race. He has even built the local synagogue at his own expense."

So Jesus set off with them. But when he was already near the house the centurion sent some personal friends with the message: "Don't put yourself to any further trouble, Lord; I am not worthy to receive you under my roof. That is why I did not presume to come in person. Just give the order and my servant will be healed. I know, because it's the same with me: although I'm only a junior officer, I have soldiers under my command. When I say to one of my men: 'Go!' he goes; when I say to another: 'Come here!' he comes; if I say to my servant: 'Do this!' he does it."

When Jesus heard that, he turned in amazement to the crowd following him and said: "I tell you I have never found faith like this, not even in Israel.

Mark my words, many people will come from the east and the west to take their places at the banquet with Abraham, Isaac and Jacob, while the kingdom's native sons will be banished into the darkness outside — that place of tears and teeth gnashing."*

Then he said to the centurion: "Go back home now; your request has been granted because of your faith."

And at that moment his servant recovered.

*A biblical expression for the disappointment, rage and despair of the damned.

CHAPTER 25

Parable of the Sower

Matthew 13:1-23; Mark 4:1-20; Luke 8:4-15

The Lakeside, November, 28 A.D.

Such big crowds surrounded Jesus one day by the lakeside that he had to get into a boat, put out to sea, and continue his teaching from there. He had many lessons for them in parables:

"A farmer went out to sow his wheat. As he sowed, some grains fell on the footpath and the birds swooped down and ate the lot. Some fell on rocky ground where there was not much soil; these sprang up quickly, but when the sun was high they were scorched by the heat and withered away, because there was no depth to their roots. Some fell among thistles, which shot up with them and smothered them, and they bore no crop. But some fell where the soil was good; these sprouted and grew and yielded a harvest — some thirty, some sixty, some a hundred times as much as was sown."

Then he sent the crowds away and went back to the house. There his disciples came to him and asked him what this parable meant.

He said to them: "The seed is the word of God. The hard ground stands for those who hear the word, but the devil comes and steals it from their hearts for fear they should believe and be saved. The rocky ground stands for those who joyfully accept the word, and yet have no real depth; they last for a time, but when trouble or persecution comes, their faith soon withers away. The thirsty ground stands for those who hear the word, but allow the cares of this world, the false glamor of riches, and the pleasures of life to smother the word, so that it remains fruitless. The good soil stands for those who hear the word and welcome it with open and generous hearts, and by their perseverance yield a harvest — some thirty, some sixty, some a hundred times as much as was sown."

THE LAKE (OR SEA) OF GALILEE

CHAPTER 26

What the Church Is Like

Matthew 13:10-15, 24-52;
Mark 4:30-34; Luke 13:18-21

The Lakeside, November, 28 A.D.

Then Jesus told a second parable: "God's kingdom is like a man who sowed clean seed in his field; but while everyone slept his enemy scattered weeds among the wheat. When the crop came into ear, the farmer's men asked him: 'Sir, didn't you sow clean seed? Where did all the weeds come from?'

" 'This is the work of an enemy.'

" 'Well, do you want us to pull the weeds up?'

" 'No. If you pull up the weeds now, you might pull up the wheat as well. Let both grow side by side until harvest time. Then I will tell the reapers to gather the weeds and burn them, but stack the wheat in my barn.'

"Again, the kingdom is like a dragnet collecting all kinds of fish from the sea. When the fishermen haul it ashore, they sit down on the beach, pick out the good ones for their cages, but throw away the worthless kind. That's how it will be at the end of the world: the angels will separate the bad from the good and throw them into the blazing furnace — that place of tears and teeth gnashing."

Here are some more parables he told them: "The kingdom is like a grain of mustard seed a man planted in his garden. Although it is the tiniest of seeds it grows bigger than any garden plant — into a tree big enough for all the birds to perch in its branches. Or, it is like a handful of yeast that a woman mixes with a sack of flour to work through it until the whole lot is leavened.

"The kingdom is like a treasure buried in a field. If a man finds it, he will hide it and joyfully sell everything he has to buy that field. Or, it is like a merchant searching for fine pearls; the moment he finds a single pearl of great value he will sell all he possesses to buy it."

Jesus spoke many more parables of this kind; it became his normal way of teaching the people, because such stories were so easy to listen to. But he always explained the meaning of the parable to his followers when they were alone by themselves, away from the crowd.

"Have you fully grasped all this?"

"Yes, Master."

"It is only to you that I am confiding the secrets of the kingdom — not to these others. Indeed, in them Isaiah's prophecy is fulfilled: 'They have closed their eyes and shut their ears; they will not come to me for healing.'

"But it's entirely different with you: you are to be the teachers and learned men of the kingdom; you must be skilled in bringing out from the treasure-house of your knowledge both the old and the new — as a rich man does."

CHAPTER 27

A Storm on the Lake

Matthew 13:53; 8:18, 23-27;
Mark 4:35-40; Luke 8:22-25

Lake of Galilee, December, 28 A.D.

That same day the crowds were still waiting on the shore at sunset — densely packed right to the water's edge.

Seeing how late it was, Jesus said to his apostles: "Let us go over to the other side of the lake."

So they said good-bye to the people and put to sea in the boat, taking Jesus along just as he was.

As they were sailing along he fell asleep in the stern. . . . Without warning a fierce windstorm swept down upon the lake, and waves broke over the boat until it was almost swamped.

They woke him up with the cry: "Master, don't you care if we all drown? Master! Master! Save us, we're sinking!"

But Jesus said to them: "Why are you such cowards, O men of little faith?"

Then, standing up to his full height, he commanded the wind and the surging waves: "Silence! Be quiet!"

At once the wind dropped and there was dead calm.

They were thunderstruck, and talked excitedly among themselves: "Who can this man really be? Why, even the wind and the sea obey his orders!"

CHAPTER 28

A Legion of Devils
Matthew 8:28-34; Mark 5:1-20;
Luke 8:26-39

Gerasa, December, 28 A.D.

So they landed on the far side of the lake, near Gerasa.

At this time the whole countryside was terrorized by a violent lunatic, possessed by the devil. He had often been chained hand and foot, but he always snapped his chains. He wore no clothes and had no home; night and day he roamed among the rock tombs and over the hillside screaming and gashing himself with rocks.

When he saw Jesus stepping ashore, he rushed up yelling and shouting and flung himself to the ground before him: "Why are you interfering, Jesus, Son of the Most High? In God's name don't torment me."

Jesus asked him: "What is your name?"

"Legion," he answered: "there are many of us."

And they implored him not to send them back to the bottomless pit, but to let them enter a herd of pigs feeding on the hillside nearby. He gave them permission. So they went into the pigs, and immediately the whole herd (about 2,000) stampeded madly down a steep slope and were drowned in the lake.

The herdsmen took to their heels and spread the news; so the people came out to see for themselves.

When they found the mad demoniac, now clothed and sane, sitting at Jesus' feet, they were gripped with such fear that they begged Jesus to leave the district.

As he was stepping into the boat, the man who had been possessed asked to go with him. But he would not allow it. "Return home to your own people," he told him, "and tell them all the Lord in his mercy has done for you."

CHAPTER 29

Miracles for Two Women
Matthew 9:1, 18-26; Mark 5:21-43;
Luke 8:40-56

Capharnaum, December, 28 A.D.

When Jesus arrived back at his hometown, he found a great crowd waiting to welcome him. He had scarcely put foot onshore when Jairus, a synagogue official, came forward and knelt down at his feet. "My only daughter is dying," he said. "Please come, lay your hands on her and save her life."

As Jesus walked along with him the crowd followed, treading on his heels. Among them was a woman suffering for twelve years from a hemorrhage. She came up behind Jesus in the crowd and touched the hem of his clothes. At that moment the source of her bleeding dried up.

Aware that power had gone out from him, Jesus turned around and said: "Somebody touched my clothes. Who was it?"

Seeing his searching eyes, the woman, scared and trembling, threw herself at his feet and told him the whole truth. But his gentle words reassured her. "Go in peace, my daughter; your faith has won this cure for you."

While he was still speaking, word came from Jairus' house that his daughter was dead. But Jesus said to him: "You have nothing to fear; only have faith."

JESUS CURES THE HEMORRHAGIC WOMAN

As they entered the house they were met with a noisy racket of flutes and wailing mourners. Jesus said to them: "There's no need for all this. The child is not dead; she is merely asleep."

They greeted this with ridicule: they had seen her dead body. But Jesus sent them all outside and went into the room where the child lay; he took her by the hand and said: "Wake up, little girl!"

There and then she came alive; she jumped to her feet and began to walk around the room — she was twelve years old. And Jesus ordered her parents, who were nearly out of their minds with joy, to give her something to eat.

CHAPTER 30

Jesus Chooses His Twelve

Matthew 10:1-33; Mark 3:13-19;
6:8-13; 13:9-13; Luke 6:12-16;
9:3-6; 12:11-12; 21:12-19

Horns of Hattin, March, 29 A.D.

About this time Jesus went out onto the hillside and spent the whole night in prayer to God. When day dawned he chose twelve of his followers to be his constant companions with authority to preach the Gospel, drive out devils, and heal the sick. He called them apostles. Here are their names:

First, Simon, called Peter, and his brother Andrew;

James the son of Zebedee and his brother John;

Philip and Bartholomew;

Thomas and Matthew the tax collector;

James the son of Cleophas and his cousin Jude;

Simon the Patriot and Judas Iscariot — the Traitor.

Before he sent the Twelve in twos on their first mission, he gave them these instructions: "Take nothing for the road except a stick to help you along; no food in your packs and no money in your pockets — not even a change of clothes or a spare pair of shoes. The workman is worth his keep.

"Are not sparrows sold two a penny? Yet not a single sparrow can fall to the ground unless your Father wills it. And as for you, why, he keeps a tally of every single hair on your head. So do not be afraid: you are more precious than a whole flock of sparrows.

"Remember, I am sending you out like sheep among a wolf pack; you will need all a snake's cunning in eluding danger — along with the childlike candor of a dove. You will be hated by all men because you bear my name; but do not let that frighten you. When they arrest you, do not worry about what you are going to say, or how to say it; words will be given you when the time comes. It is not *you* that speak; it's the Spirit of your Father speaking through you.

"Whoever stands up for me in this life, I, too, will stand up for him in my heavenly Father's presence on Judgment Day; but whoever disowns me before men, before my heavenly Father I, too, will disown him."

Chapter 31

Trust in God's Fatherly Care
Matthew 6:19-34;
Luke 12:15-34; 16:13

Plain of Sharon, December, 29 A.D.

"Do not be afraid, my little flock; your Father plans to give you his kingdom.

"You cannot serve God and money. So sell all your possessions and give the money away. Acquire never-failing heavenly credit, a treasure that will never grow rusty or moth-eaten, that no thief can rob you of. Where your treasure is, there, too, your heart is bound to be.

"So stop worrying yourselves with anxious doubts. Don't be always asking: 'What are we to eat? What are we to drink? What are we going to wear?' Let the pagans run after those things. But not you: *you* have a Father in heaven who knows all your needs.

"Look at the birds on the wing! They don't sow or reap or store the harvest in barns, and yet your heavenly Father feeds them. Are not you much more precious to him than they? Can any of you, no matter how much he worries, add a day to his life? Seeing you cannot alter so small a thing, why worry about your other needs?

"And why be anxious about clothes? See how the wild flowers grow! They don't do one bit of work, yet not even Solomon in all his splendor was robed as finely as one of these. If God so clothes the grass, which blossoms in the field today and feeds the furnace tomorrow, will he not be much more ready to clothe you, O men of little faith?

"Be on your guard against greed of every kind; a man's life does not consist in having more possessions than he needs. . . . Once there was a rich man whose lands yielded a heavy crop. So he decided to pull down his barns and build bigger ones. He thought that with all his wealth stored up he could relax for years to come — eating, drinking and having a good time.

"But God said: 'You fool, this very night you must die, and someone else will get all your money.'

"That's how it is with the man who amasses wealth for himself; he is a pauper in God's sight.

"No, set your heart on winning God's kingdom; then all these extras will be thrown in as a matter of course. Never worry about tomorrow; tomorrow will take care of itself. Take each day's troubles as they come."

Chapter 32

Parable of the Talents
Matthew 25:14-30
Bethany, April, 30 A.D.

"The kingdom is like a man going abroad who sent for the members of his household and handed his fortune over to them to manage. He gave five talents* to one, two to another, and one to a third — to each one according to his capacity. Then he left the country.

"The man who had received five talents traded with them until he had made another five. So did the man with two; he made another two. But the man with the one merely dug a hole in the ground and buried his master's money.

"The master at last came back and proceeded to settle accounts with them. The man who had received five brought him an extra five. 'Lord,' he said, 'you gave me five talents; look, I've made five more!' And the master replied: 'Well done, my good and trusted servant! Seeing you have been trustworthy in small things, now I have something big to entrust to you: a sharing in your Lord's own happiness.'

"Next came the man who had received two talents. 'Lord,' he said, 'you gave me two talents; look, I've made two more!' And his master replied: 'Well done, my good and trusted servant! Seeing you have

*A bar of gold or silver weighing about 100 pounds.

been trustworthy in small things, now I have something big to entrust to you: a sharing in your Lord's own happiness.'

"Last of all the man with one single talent made his statement: 'Lord, I always knew you for a hard man; so I was afraid. I buried your talent in the ground; here's your money back again intact.'

"And his master replied: 'You lazy, good-for-nothing servant! You ought to have put my money in the bank so that I could have got back what belongs to me with interest. . . . Take the talent away from him and give it to the man with ten talents. And now throw this useless servant into the darkness outside — that place of tears and teeth gnashing.' "

CHAPTER 33

The Vine and Its Branches
John 15:1-16
The Cenacle, Thursday,
April 6, 30 A.D.

"I am the vine, the true vine; and my Father is the gardener. He cuts off any barren branches, but prunes the fruitful ones to make them bear still more. You have been pruned already by my purifying teaching; remain then united to me, as I am to you. Just as the branch can bear no fruit unless it shares the life of the vine, so you can produce nothing unless you go on growing in me.

"I am the vine, you are my branches; anyone who remains united to me, and I to him, will yield abundant fruit; separated from me you can do nothing at all. If a man does not share my life, he is like a branch that is broken off and withers away. But if you live your life in me, and my teachings live on in your hearts, you can ask for anything you wish and you shall have it. When you yield abundant fruit and prove to be true disciples, my Father is indeed honored.

"I have loved you just as my Father has loved me. My love must be your life: it is by keeping my commandments that you will go on living in my love, just as I live in my Father's love by keeping his commandments. This is my very own commandment: Love one another as I have loved you. To die for one's friends — that is the greatest love of all; yet you are my friends if you do what I tell you. I shall not call you servants anymore: a servant is not taken into his master's confidence. No, I am calling you friends now, because I have shared all my Father's secrets with you.

"You did not choose me; it was I that chose you, and appointed you to go out and bear fruit — everlasting fruit. I assure you that *whatever* you ask the Father in my name, he will give it to you."

CHAPTER 34

Jesus' Prayer for His Apostles
John 17:1-26

The Cenacle, Thursday,
April 6, 30 A.D.*

When they had sung the hymn of praise, Jesus prayed with eyes raised to heaven: "Father, I have made your divine person known to the men you entrusted to me — men chosen out of the world. They were yours, but you gave them to me, and they obeyed your command.

"Now they realize that everything I possess comes from you alone. I have handed on the message you gave me; they have accepted it and have come to know in their hearts that I came from you; they have found faith to believe that you sent me. These are the men I am praying for — *your* men. But since we share all, they are mine, too — my crowning glory.

"The end of my mortal life is near; but they must stay on while I return to you. Holy Father, please keep them loyal to your person, so that they may be one in us: as you, Father, are in me, and I in you. As long as I was with them I kept them loyal to you; but while I am still in the world I am telling them this, so that the happiness I myself feel may be fully realized in their own hearts.

"I have given them your message, and the world

*Cf. Chapter 56.

has nothing but hatred for them, because they do not belong to it anymore than I do. I am not asking you to take them out of the world, but to preserve them from its evil influence. Please keep them holy then, united to the truth — your word is truth. Just as you sent me as your ambassador, so I am sending them into the world as my ambassadors, and am offering myself as a victim for their sakes that they, too, may be completely dedicated witnesses to the truth.

"I am not praying for them only; I am praying also for those who will believe in me through their preaching. My prayer is that they may all be united together — united in us, just as you, Father, are in me and I in you. May they all be one, as we are one: I, living in them, as you are in me.

"Father, this is my great desire: May everyone entrusted to my care on earth be with me in heaven contemplating the glory that is mine from all eternity. Father, dear Father, I have made known, and will continue to make known, your will to them; so that your tremendous love for me may dwell in their hearts — and I may be there also."

CHAPTER 35

Bread and Fish Multiplied

Matthew 14:13-21; Mark 6:31-44;
Luke 9:10-17; John 6:1-15

Near Bethsaida, April, 29 A.D.

Jesus once sent his apostles out on a missionary
tour of Galilee; on their return he said to them:
"Come along now to some quiet place for a few days'
rest."

So they went off by boat across the lake in the di-
rection of Bethsaida. But many saw them going and
guessed their destination; hurrying to the place on
foot they arrived before them.

Jesus' heart went out to these people — sheep
without a shepherd. So he spoke to them for a long
time about the kingdom of God, and cured all the
sick.

It was getting late when the Twelve came to him
and said: "You'd better dismiss the crowd now so
they can go and buy food for themselves — we're
right out in the wilds here."

Jesus replied: "There's no need for them to go
away: *you* give them something to eat."

Philip answered: "Why, it would take 200
dinars* to provide each person with just one mouth-
ful!"

*The Roman denarius, a silver coin equal to a day's
wages. Dinar, incidentally, is the present-day name for the
Jordanian pound.

THE MIRACLE OF THE LOAVES OF BREAD AND FISH

Jesus said: "Find out how many loaves of bread you have."

Andrew replied: "There's a youngster here with five barley loaves and a couple of smoked fish; but what use is that for such a crowd?"

"Bring them here to me," Jesus commanded; "and tell the people to sit down in groups on the green grass."

He then took the five loaves and the two fish in his hands and looked up to heaven; after saying grace he broke the loaves into portions, which he kept on handing to his apostles who served the crowd. He also distributed the fish in the same way — as much as everyone wanted.

As the full meaning of this wonderful sign began to dawn on the 5,000 guests (not counting women and children) a growing number of excited voices was heard: "This man undoubtedly is the Prophet the world has been waiting for!"

Chapter 36

Jesus Walks on the Water
Matthew 14:22-33; Mark 6:45-52;
John 6:16-21

Lake of Galilee, April, 29 A.D.

Realizing that they meant to carry him off and make him their king, Jesus ordered his apostles to take the boat and go on ahead of him, while he sent the crowds home. After he had dismissed them he climbed up alone into the hillside to pray.

Meanwhile his apostles went down to the lake and started to cross the water to Capharnaum, passing near Bethsaida. Night fell and Jesus had not yet come back to them. A strong wind sprang up and the sea quickly grew rough; driven by the wind and the waves, the boat was soon out in the middle of the lake.

In the early hours, seeing them straining at the oars (they had rowed some three or four miles into the wind), Jesus came to them walking on the water. When they caught sight of him coming toward the boat, the apostles were terrified. "It's a ghost!" they said, as they cried out with fear.

But at once Jesus spoke to them: "Have confidence! It's only myself; there's nothing to be afraid of."

Reassured, Peter said to him: "Lord, if it's *really* you, tell me to come to you over the water."

"Come," replied Jesus.

Peter stepped down from the boat and began walking over the waves, heading toward Jesus. But when he felt the fury of the gale he panicked. As he began to sink he called out: "Quick, Lord, save me!"

Jesus at once stretched out his hand and caught hold of him, saying: "Why did you doubt, O man of little faith?"

As he stepped into the boat the wind suddenly dropped; and the apostles went down on their knees to him, saying: "You are truly the Son of God."

CHAPTER 37

Jesus Promises Himself as Food
John 6:22-72

Capharnaum Synagogue,
April, 29 A.D.

When the crowd found him after he had crossed the lake, they asked him: "Master, when did you make your way here?"

Jesus answered: "You have come looking for me only because I provided you with bread — mere perishable food! You should be more interested in finding food that lasts forever: the Son of Man can give you this kind of food, too."

They said: "That's the food we want — all the time!"

Jesus replied: "I myself am that life-giving food; he who comes to me with faith will never be hungry or thirsty again. If anyone eats the living food that has come down from heaven, he shall live forever. What sort of food is this? My own flesh given up in sacrifice to bring the world back to life."

This led to a heated discussion among the Jews: "How can this man give us his flesh?" they argued.

Jesus then said: "I am only telling you the plain truth: unless you eat the flesh of the Son of Man and drink his blood you are not truly alive; but the man who eats my flesh and drinks my blood already possesses eternal life, because my flesh and blood are real food and drink — true nourishment. Just as I have life from the living Father, so he who is nourished by me will live with my life."

As a consequence many of his followers would no longer associate with him. So Jesus said to the Twelve: "*You* don't want to go away, too, do you?"

Simon Peter spoke up: "Go away, Lord? Who else is there to go to? We firmly believe, we are fully convinced, that *you* are the Holy One of God."

Jesus replied: "Didn't I choose you myself — all twelve of you? And yet one of you has the devil in his heart."

CHAPTER 38

Peter's Profession of Faith
Matthew 16:5-19; Mark 8:14-29;
Luke 9:18-20; 22:31-32

Caesarea Philippi, July, 29 A.D.

One day when Jesus was crossing the lake by boat with his apostles, he warned them to have nothing to do with the leaven of the Pharisees. They thought he was speaking of leavened bread (they had forgotten to bring any bread with them); but his warning was really against the doctrine of the Pharisees, not against baker's leaven.

When they arrived at Bethsaida a blind man was brought to him to be cured. Jesus led him by the hand away from the town, touched his eyes with spittle, and asked: "Can you see anything now?"

As his sight came back gradually he said: "I can see some things like trees; no, they're moving about! They must be men, then."

Once more Jesus laid his hands on his eyes, so that his sight was completely restored.

Then Jesus went with his apostles toward Caesarea Philippi. In a lonely place along the road, after he had spent some time in prayer, he asked them: "What's the general opinion about the Son of Man? Who do people think he is?"

They said, "Well, some say John the Baptist, others Elijah or Jeremiah, still others that one of the ancient prophets has returned to life."

"And you? Who do *you* say I am?"

Then Simon Peter spoke up: "You are the Messiah. You are the Son of the living God."

At this Jesus declared: "Simon, son of John,* you are a privileged man indeed! It is my heavenly Father who has made this revelation to you — no human power could. And now I have a message for you personally: you are Peter† [*Kepha*] and upon this rock [*kepha*] I will build my church; the mighty forces of evil shall be powerless against it.

"And I will give you the keys of the kingdom: any decision you make on earth will be ratified by God in heaven above."

Later on Jesus said to Peter: "O Simon, dear Simon, Satan has obtained permission to shake all of you like wheat in a sieve; but I have prayed for you, Simon, that your faith may never fail. And you, once you have repented, are to be the strong support of all the faithful."

*Literally *Bar-Jona*, but intended perhaps to sound as a play on the Aramaic word meaning impulsive, unrestrained. Those who through lack of self-control were openly hostile to Rome were called *barjonim*.

†Both *Peter* and *rock* are the same word in Aramaic. This is the first time a human being was ever so named (see Chapter 11).

CHAPTER 39

A Glimpse of Christ's Glory
Matthew 16:21—17:8;
Mark 8:31—9:7; Luke 9:22-36
Mount Hermon, August, 29 A.D.

Now for the first time Jesus told his apostles: "The Son of Man must go up to Jerusalem, be rejected by the Jewish leaders, and put to death; but he will rise again on the third day."

Then he called the people and said to them: "If anyone wishes to walk in my footsteps, he must trample on self, shoulder his cross daily, and follow me. Whoever tries to save his life will lose it anyway; but he who loses his life for my sake will save it in the end. What use is it for a man to gain the whole world if he loses his own soul?"

A week later Jesus took Peter, James and John with him and climbed a high, remote mountain to pray. And as he prayed his whole appearance was transformed: his face became radiant as the sun, his clothes a dazzling white — bright as a flash of lightning. Suddenly two men appeared in a blaze of glory; they were Moses and Elijah announcing the triumph of his death in Jerusalem.

Although drowsy with sleep, Peter and his companions stayed awake, gazing at his glory and the two men with him. As they began to move away from Jesus, Peter blurted out: "Master, it is a good thing we are here; if you wish, we can quickly put up three shelters — one for you, one for Elijah and one for Moses." But he didn't really know what he was saying.

While he was still talking a luminous cloud covered them with its shadow, filling them with awe as it enveloped the others. From the cloud a voice rang out: "This is my Son, my Chosen One; be sure and listen to him."

At the sound of the voice the apostles fell flat on their faces, overcome with fear. But Jesus approached and placed his hand on them: "Stand up now," he said; "there's no need to be afraid."

They looked up then and saw no one but Jesus — all alone.

CHAPTER 40

"One Flock and One Shepherd"
John 10:1-18
Bethany, November, 29 A.D.

"You know well that the man who climbs into the sheepfold by any other way than the gate is a thief and a robber; a true shepherd always comes in through the gate. The sheep at once recognize his voice as he calls them by name; when he has collected all his own flock he walks ahead of them, and they follow him because they know his voice. They will never follow a stranger; on the contrary, they will run away from him, because they don't recognize the voice of strangers."

This was a parable Jesus told the Pharisees; but they did not know what he meant. So he explained it: "I am the entrance gate. A man will be an approved shepherd only if he makes his way in through me; then he can come and go freely, and find pasture for his sheep. All the rest are thieves and robbers; that is why the sheep take no notice of them. The thief only comes to steal, to slaughter, to destroy; I have come to bring men life — abundant and everlasting life.

"I am the good shepherd, too. The good shepherd lays down his life for his sheep; but the hired man deserts the sheep and runs away as soon as he sees the wolf coming, because he is no shepherd and the sheep are not his; and so the wolf attacks and scatters them.

"I am the good shepherd. I know and love my sheep and they me, just as my Father knows and loves me and I him. To save these sheep of mine I will lay down my life. Nobody can take it away from me; I am making the offering of my own free will. I have power to lay it down, and power to take it up again.

"I must have other sheep, too, not yet members of the fold. I must also lead them out to pasture as well, so that they can listen to my voice; and then there will be one flock, one shepherd."

CHAPTER 41

Jesus Entrusts His Flock to Peter

Luke 24:36-43;
John 20:19-23; 21:4-23

**Jerusalem and Galilee,
April-May, 30 A.D.**

It was late on Sunday evening. For fear of the Jews the apostles had bolted the doors of the room in which they had assembled. As they sat talking at table, Jesus came and stood there among them. "Peace be in your hearts," he said. "As my Father has made me his ambassador, so now I am going to hand on this same mission to you."

With that he breathed on them and said: "Receive the Holy Spirit. When you forgive men's sins, they are forgiven; when you refuse forgiveness, unforgiven they remain."

Later on Jesus appeared at daybreak to a group of apostles out fishing on the lake.* After breakfast he said to Simon Peter: "Simon, son of John, are you more devoted to me than all the others?"

"Yes, Lord, I *do* love you — you know I do."

"Then feed my lambs."

Again a second time he asked: "Simon, son of John, are you truly my friend?"

*For details of this scene, see Chapter 69.

97

"Yes, Lord, of course I am; you know I love you."

"Then take care of my young sheep."

For the third time he asked: "Simon, son of John, do you *really* love me?"

Peter was deeply hurt at being asked the same question three times over and said: "Lord, you know everything; you can see the love in my heart."

"Then feed my sheep."

On the hillside Jesus later spoke to all his apostles: "Absolute authority has been committed to me in heaven and on earth. Go out then all over the world and preach the gospel to all nations; baptize them in the name of the Father and the Son and the Holy Spirit, teaching them to observe all the commandments I have given you. And remember I will *always* be with you — right till the end of time."

MAP OF THE LAST JOURNEY OF JESUS

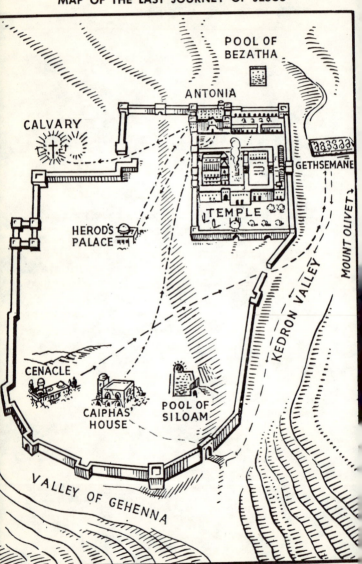

PART 3

Death on a Cross and Victorious Resurrection

In this final portion of our Lord's life the apostles fade into the background. Jesus walks alone to his death. He has founded his church on Peter, and trained the Twelve in the guidance and government of the kingdom. His whole mind and purpose is now centered on the last act of the drama: his own death on the cross that will set men free forever from the domination of sin and Satan.

The stage for our Lord's personal act of atonement is Jerusalem (only two of the thirty-one scenes in this Part are located away from the city — Chapters 46 and 69), the Holy City that was the very heart and soul of Israel's life. It is a different world from Galilee (Part 2): the bright, blue lake is now replaced by the hard, stone walls of the proud city seated majestically in the Judean hills.

The happy, enthusiastic crowds of the lakeside give way to the cold, hostile Jewish leaders who dominate the scene in Jerusalem. They are the Pharisees and Sadducees, men of learning and power, who summarily reject Jesus the moment he sets foot in the Temple. They recognize right from the start that he is a threat to their position, and they oppose him with a fierce, unreasoning hatred.

About half of the scenes of this section (Chapters 51 to 65) are taken up with the last day of our Lord's life on earth: from the Last Supper on Thursday evening (the Jewish day began at sunset) till his burial at the foot of Calvary late on Friday afternoon. This is the great, solemn day (the 14th of Nisan) of the most important Jewish festival (Passover). The year is probably 30 A.D.

Jesus himself was the paschal lamb offered in sacrifice to the Father for the world's sins. By his death he won life for all men. He showed this by his Resurrection, which is not only a proof of his divinity, but also the completion of our salvation. By baptism we are built into and become members of a living, risen Christ: we are not incorporated into a corpse! "Jesus our Lord was put to death for our sins, and raised from the dead to bring us back to life" (Romans 4:25).

CHAPTER 42

Racketeers Driven from the Temple

John 2:13-22; Matthew 21:12-13
Mark 11:15-18; Luke 19:45-48

The Temple, March, 28 A.D.

The paschal feast was approaching, so Jesus made the journey to Jerusalem. There in the Temple he came upon the dealers buying and selling cattle, sheep and pigeons — and money changers sitting at their tables.

So he made a rough whip out of rope and drove the whole lot (men, sheep and cattle) out of the Temple; he sent the coins of the bankers flying and turned their tables upside down — and the chairs of the pigeon sellers as well. And he stopped those transporting goods across the sacred enclosure, as though it were a public street.

Then he said to the pigeon sellers: "Take them out of here. Don't you dare make a marketplace of my Father's house! Scripture says: 'My house shall be a place of *prayer* for all nations.' And look what *you* are doing! You're turning it into 'a den of thieves.' "

The Jewish leaders challenged him: "What right have you to act like this? We want proof of your authority."

"Proof!" replied Jesus. "Destroy this shrine and I will raise it up again within three days."

JESUS DRIVES OUT THE RACKETEERS

The Jewish leaders retorted: "It took forty-six years to build this shrine; how could *you* put it up again in three days?"

(But the shrine he meant, of course, was his own body. So afterwards, when he had risen from the dead, his followers remembered what he had said, and were convinced of the truth of Sacred Scripture and of Jesus' own prophecy.)

As a result of this the chief priests and lawyers began racking their brains for ways and means of doing away with him; but they were afraid to act because of his popularity with the people.

CHAPTER 43

A Cripple at the Pool
John 5:1-47
The Temple, April, 29 A.D.

One sabbath day Jesus was passing through the archways around the Bezatha pool in Jerusalem. Crowds of sick people were waiting there for the water to start bubbling (they believed that an angel came down from time to time and stirred up the water, and that the first into the bubbling water would be cured).

Among them was a man crippled for thirty-eight years. Jesus seeing him lying there went over to him and asked: "Do you want to get well again?"

"Sir," said the cripple, "I just have not anyone to help me down into the pool when the water is all stirred up; somebody else always gets in before me."

"Stand up!" Jesus said to him. "Pick up your mat and walk!"

There and then the man was cured; he picked up his mat and began to walk.

This breach of sabbath observance stirred up the Jewish leaders to prosecute Jesus. He answered their charge by saying: "Every day of the week is a work-day for my Father; and so it must be for me, too."

This remark made them more determined than ever to kill him; by calling God his *own* Father he was actually claiming *equality* with God.

So Jesus continued his defense: "The Son cannot

do anything on his own authority; he can do only what he sees his Father doing. Just as the Father brings the dead back to life, so, too, the Son can give life to anyone he chooses. Anyone who heeds my message, and puts his trust in him who sent me, is already in possession of eternal life; he has passed once and for all from death to life.

"You read the scriptures over and over again, thinking to find eternal life in them; and, in fact, it is precisely these same scriptures that point me out to you; yet you will not come to me, the source of life, because you have not the love of God in your hearts."

CHAPTER 44

"Before Abraham Was, I Am"

Luke 9:51;
John 7:2, 25-26, 12; 8:31-59

The Temple, October, 29 A.D.

The time was getting close now for Jesus to be taken away from this earth, so he turned his face resolutely toward the road leading to Jerusalem. He arrived in the Temple during the Festival of Tents and began teaching.

Some of the people expressed surprise at his coming. "Isn't this the man they want to kill? Yet here he is speaking right out in the open, and they haven't a word to say to him! Can it be our leaders now realize he is the Messiah?"

Jesus began to speak: "I am the light of the world. Whoever follows me will never wander about in the dark; he will possess the light that is life itself. . . . If you carry out my teaching, you are truly my disciples; then you will come to know the truth — truth that will make you free men."

They answered: "We are Abraham's descendants; nobody has ever made slaves of us."

Jesus replied: "Yes, I know you are Abraham's race; but you are not true children of his, because you are planning to kill me, a man who simply told you the truth, as God the Father revealed it to me. If you are Abraham's *true* children, why don't you follow his example?"

They said: "We are no apostates; we are faithful sons of our one and only Father — God."

Jesus told them: "If God were your Father, you would welcome me into your hearts; I am his Son and ambassador. . . . If anyone obeys my teaching, he will never die."

The Jewish leaders took him up: "Now we're sure you are possessed by the devil. What of Abraham and the prophets? All of them are dead; yet you declare that a man will never die if he obeys your teaching. Are *you* a greater man than our father Abraham? Even *he* had to die — and so did the prophets, too. Who do you think *you* are?"

Jesus answered: "If I were trying to glorify myself, such glory would be worthless; but it is the Father who glorifies me. As for your father Abraham, he was filled with joy at the thought of my coming. Yes, the sight of that day gladdened his heart."

"How can *you* have seen Abraham? Why, you're not yet fifty years old!"

"What I now tell you is solemn truth: Before Abraham was, *I Am*."

At this they picked up stones to throw at him; but he disappeared in the crowd and made his way out of the Temple unobserved.

CHAPTER 45

"My Father and I Are One"
John 10:22-42;
Matthew 19:1-2; Mark 10:1

The Temple, December, 29 A.D.

So Jesus journeyed through the towns and villages of Judea teaching. Then once more he took the road back to Jerusalem for the Dedication Feast.

It was wintertime, and as he was walking up and down in Solomon's Cloister the Jewish leaders closed in on him and demanded: "How long are you going to keep us in suspense? If you *really* are the Messiah, tell us so in plain words."

He replied: "I *have* told you, but you refuse to believe me. All that I have done in my Father's name is sufficient proof of my claim; and still you will not believe me, because you are not sheep of my flock. My sheep listen to my voice and follow me. I give them everlasting life; and no one can take that away from them. The Father has entrusted them to my care; no one can take anything by force from my Father — he is all-powerful. My Father and I are one."

Again the Jewish leaders took up stones and were ready to put him to death. But Jesus remonstrated with them: "You have witnessed many acts of mercy which my Father has given me power to do for your benefit; for which particular one do you intend to stone me?"

"We're not going to stone you for any act of

kindness, but for blasphemy: you claim to be *God* — you, a mere man!"

"You accuse me of blasphemy because I called myself God's Son. Well, if you find that I'm not acting like my Father's true Son should, then put no trust in me; but if I am, then let my actions convince you where I myself cannot, so you will come to realize once and for all that the Father is in me, and I in him."

Once more they tried to arrest him; but he slipped through their hands and went back across the Jordan river. Big crowds came out to him; and he taught them there — as he always did.

CHAPTER 46

The Lost Son Comes Back Home
Luke 15:1-3, 11-32
Jordan Valley, February, 30 A.D.

When the Pharisees noticed so many tax collectors and outcasts approaching to listen to him, they were most indignant and muttered: "Look at him! He not only welcomes sinners; he even takes his meals with them!"

So he told them this story: "Once there was a man who had two sons. One day the younger one said, 'Father, give me my share of the family fortune.'

"So the father divided up all his wealth between the two sons.

"The younger lost no time in packing all his belongings and setting out for a distant country, where he wasted his fortune in prodigal dissipation. And when a severe famine came he faced starvation. So he went to work for a local landowner, who sent him out on his farm to herd pigs. He was so hungry he would willingly have eaten the same food as the pigs; but nobody gave him a thing — not even pig food!

"At last he came to his senses. 'Why,' he said to himself, 'there are dozens of workmen employed by my father who have more food than they can eat, while here I am starving to death! I will leave this place and go back this very minute to my father and say to him, "Father, I've sinned against God and against you; I don't deserve to be called your son anymore; please take me back and I will work for my keep." '

"There and then he started back home to his father. While still a long way off, his father saw him coming and his heart went out to him. He ran out to meet him, threw his arms around him, and kissed him tenderly.

"No sooner had the son begun his confession than the father gave orders to the servants: 'Hurry up now! Go and get him new clothes — the very best in the house. Put a ring on his finger, and shoes on his feet. Then go and kill the fattened calf: we will have a party to celebrate the homecoming of my son. I thought he was dead, and here he is alive! I thought I had lost him, and I've found him again!'

"But his elder brother disapproved angrily, saying: 'Look, I have served you all these years and never once have I disobeyed your orders, and you have never given me even a kid to enjoy myself with my friends. But no sooner does this son of yours come, having squandered your estate with harlots, than you kill the fattened calf for him.'

" 'But son,' he said to him, 'you are always with me, and all that I have is yours. Surely we should make merry and rejoice, because this brother of yours was dead and is alive again; he was lost and is found.' "

CHAPTER 47

Jesus Raises Lazarus from the Dead

John 11:1-54

Bethany, March, 30 A.D.

At Bethany a man lay dying, he was Lazarus, the brother of Martha and Mary. The sisters sent a message to Jesus: "Lord, do you know your dear friend is ill?"

By the time he arrived, Lazarus was four days dead. As soon as Martha heard Jesus was on his way, she went out to meet him. "Lord, if only you had been here," she said, "my brother would not have died."

"Your brother will rise again."

"Yes, I know he will rise again at the resurrection on the Last Day."

"I am the resurrection; I am life itself. He who believes in me, even if he is dead, will live on; anyone who lives and believes in me does not really die at all. You believe this, don't you?"

"Yes, Lord, I've always believed that you are the Messiah, the Son of God; it is for your coming the whole world has been waiting."

With that she went back to the house and whispered to Mary: "The Master is here; he's asking for you."

The moment Mary heard this she was on her feet, running to him. When Jesus saw her kneeling at his feet crying her eyes out (and her companions also weeping), he breathed a deep sigh that made him shudder. "Where have you buried him?" he asked.

Then Jesus himself broke into silent tears. Still visibly shaken he came to the grave; it was a cave with a stone slab over the mouth. "Take away the stone," he said.

Then he raised his eyes to heaven in prayer and called out in a commanding voice: "Lazarus, come to me — out here!"

At once the dead man came out, hands and feet securely tied with cords — even the chinband still over his head.

Many of those who witnessed this miracle of Jesus became believers; but some of them went off and reported it to the Jewish leaders.

They at once summoned a council meeting, saying: "We must take action at once; if we leave him alone, everyone will believe in him. Then the Romans will have an excuse to take over and put an end to our national existence."

The high priest Caiphas said: "Better that one man die for the people than that the whole nation be destroyed."

From that day they began plotting his death. So Jesus made no further public appearances; he withdrew to Ephrem, a town in the country, with his followers.

CHAPTER 48

The King on a Donkey

Matthew 20:17-19; 21:1-9; Mark
10:32-34; 11:1-10; Luke 18:31-34;
19:29-44; John 12:12-19

**Mount Olivet, Sunday,
April 2, 30 A.D.**

Then one day Jesus gathered his Twelve around
him and said to them solemnly: "Listen carefully. We
are now going up to Jerusalem, where the Son of
Man will be betrayed to the chief priests and lawyers,
condemned to death, and handed over to the hea-
then; they will humiliate him, spit in his face, flog him
and kill him. But three days later he will rise from the
dead."

A week before the paschal feast began Jesus arrived at Bethany. Next day he sent two of his apostles
with these instructions: "Go into that village over
there and you will find a donkey standing in the
street, tied up near a gate; bring it back here to me."
(This was done to make the prophet's words come
true: "Look, daughter of Sion, here comes your
King, humbly riding on a donkey.")

So they brought the colt to Jesus, threw their
cloaks on as a saddle, and invited him to mount it. A
big crowd, up for the festival, hearing that Jesus was
on his way into Jerusalem, went out to escort him in,
waving palm branches and singing God's praises for
all the wonders they had seen him do. They spread

116

their cloaks on the roadway, cut green branches from the olive trees, and carpeted his path with them. The moment they topped the hill a mighty shout went up: "Hosanna! God bless Israel's King; God bless David's Son. The kingdom has come at last. Hurrah!"

At this some of the Pharisees among the crowd said to him: "Rabbi, restrain your followers."

But he replied: "If they were to stop, the very stones on the road would start cheering."

As he came nearer, Jesus suddenly caught sight of the city and wept over it, saying: "If only you, too, on this great day could find the road that leads to peace! But no, the day is coming when your enemies will beat you flat to the ground, because you did not recognize your moment of grace."

CHAPTER 49

Parable of the Murderous Sharecroppers

Matthew 21:33-46; Mark 12:1-12; Luke 20:9-19

The Temple, Tuesday, April 4, 30 A.D.

Each evening Jesus went back to Bethany, returning to the Temple early in the morning and teaching there all day. All the people hung upon his words. This is one of the stories he told them:

"Once there was a rich landowner who planted a vineyard; he put a stone wall around it, dug a wine vat out of the solid rock, built a watch tower, and then leased it to sharecroppers, while he went away to spend a long time abroad. When the grapes were ripe he sent an agent to collect his share of the crop. But the sharecroppers beat him up and sent him away emptyhanded. The owner tried again and again with many other agents; but the sharecroppers threw them all out of the vineyard, sometimes wounding, sometimes stoning — even murdering some of them.

"So the owner of the vineyard thought to himself: 'What shall I do *now*? There's only my son left, my only son, so dear to me. I will send *him*; surely they will respect my son.'

"As soon as the sharecroppers saw the son coming they put their heads together: 'This is the heir;

come on, let us kill him and we will own everything ourselves.' So they seized hold of him, threw him out of the vineyard, and killed him.

"And now, what do you suppose the owner will do to those sharecroppers when he returns? He will destroy those murderers and lease his vineyard to new tenants who will pay him his share of the crop, season after season. Mark my words: the kingdom of God will be taken away from you and handed over to other people; *they* will make it pay!"

The chief priests and Pharisees saw clearly, when they heard this story, that he was speaking about them. They wanted to arrest him there and then, but were afraid of the people who looked on him as a prophet.

CHAPTER 50

Jesus Denounces the Hypocrisy of the Pharisees

Matthew 22:15-22; 23:23-38; Mark
12:13-17; Luke 20:20-26; 13:34-35

The Temple, Tuesday,
April 4, 30 A.D.

The Pharisees went off and plotted together how
to trap him in his own words and then hand him over
to the supreme authority of the Roman governor.
They sent their spies (who pretended to be honest
men) to put this question to him: "Rabbi, we know
you're frank and not afraid of anyone. Please give us
your ruling: Is it right or wrong to pay our taxes to
Caesar?"

Jesus saw their malice. "Let me see one of the
coins you pay in taxation," he said.

So they handed him a dinar. He asked: "Whose
image is this? Whose name is inscribed on the coin?"

"Caesar's," they replied.

"Then you must pay back to Caesar what is Caesar's, and to God what is God's," he answered. . . .

"What doom awaits you, lawyers and Pharisees,
you hypocrites! You pay your ten percent tax on
mint, anise and cummin, but disregard the more important obligations of the law: justice, mercy and
good faith. You strain off the mosquito [*kalama*] and
then swallow the camel [*gamala*]!

"What doom awaits you, lawyers and Pharisees, you hypocrites! You are like whitewashed tombs: outwardly attractive, but inside full of rottenness and dead men's bones. You look like good men, but you're riddled with hypocrisy and evil. You blind guides! You serpents! You snake pack! How can you hope to escape the damnation of hell?

"O Jerusalem, Jerusalem, you murderess and prophet killer! Again and again I have longed to gather your children to me as a hen gathers her chickens under her wings; but you turned your back on me. Very well then: you can now have your house all to yourselves — a *deserted* house."

**THE COIN OF TRIBUTE, AFTER TITIAN
(ARTIST UNKNOWN)**

CHAPTER 51

Jesus Washes His Apostles' Feet

Matthew 26:1-5, 14-16, 20, 29;
Mark 14:1-2, 10-11, 17, 25; 10:45;
Luke 22:1-6, 14-18, 24; John 13:1-15

The Cenacle, 6 p.m., Thursday, April 6, 30 A.D.

While the Jewish officials were discussing ways and means of getting Jesus into their power, Judas Iscariot, one of the Twelve, came to them with a plan: "*I* will hand him over to you," he said. "How much will you pay me?"

They listened eagerly to what he had to say and willingly agreed to pay him thirty shekels* — provided he handed Jesus over in the absence of a crowd.

On the day before the paschal feast, at sunset, Jesus came to an upstairs room and sat down at table with his twelve apostles. He said to them: "How eagerly I have waited for this day, longed with all my heart to eat this last Passover with you! Today the symbol will be replaced by the reality it stood for."

As they were taking their places at table an argument started: which of them had the right to the top seats? So Jesus stood up, took off his cloak, and wrapped a towel around his waist; then he poured

---

*A shekel was a Jewish coin, four times the value of a Roman denarius (cf. Chapters 35 and 50).

water into a basin and began to wash and dry their feet.

When he came to Simon Peter, that apostle spoke up: "Master, you're surely not going to wash my feet? Not *you*, Lord!"

"Yes, Peter. You don't understand now why I'm doing this; but one day you will."

"No, Lord, never! I wouldn't dream of letting *you* wash my feet."

"If I don't wash you, it means you cannot share anything with me again."

"In that case, Lord, please wash my hands and my face as well — not just my feet."

When Jesus had washed their feet he put on his cloak and sat down again at table. Then he said to them: "Since I, the Lord and Master, have washed your feet, you, too, must be ready to wash one another's feet. That is the lesson I have just given you. Never forget that the Son of Man did not come on earth to be waited on; he came to serve others and to give his life as a ransom for the whole of mankind."

CHAPTER 52

The Last Supper

Matthew 26:21-28; Mark 14:18-24;
Luke 22:21-23, 19-20; John 13:21-30,
34-35; 1 Corinthians 11:23-25

The Cenacle, 7 p.m., Thursday, April 6, 30 A.D.

Right at the beginning of the meal Jesus made known the deep distress he felt in his heart: "One of you is going to betray me; the traitor's hand rests on this table, alongside mine."

Sick at heart, the apostles looked at one another, completely mystified: "It is not I, Lord, is it?" they asked him sadly, each in turn.

Peter attracted the attention of John, who was sitting next to Jesus, and whispered: "Find out who it is he means."

This apostle simply leaned back and rested his head on Jesus' shoulder and asked: "Lord, who is it?"

Jesus answered: "The man I'm going to pass this handful of herbs to." He picked up a handful, dipped it in the sauce, and handed it to Judas Iscariot.

Then Judas said brazenly: "Rabbi, it's surely not *I?*"

"Yes, it *is* you," Jesus answered.

This was the moment Satan took possession of Judas.

Then Jesus said to him out loud: "Be quick in doing what you have to do."

Immediately Judas got up and went out — into the night.

Jesus had always loved those who belonged to him; now he would show the infinite depths of his love. He took a loaf of bread, said grace, broke it into pieces, and handed it to his apostles: "Take it, eat it; this is my body, given up in sacrifice for you."

Then, at the end of the meal, he did the same with a cup of wine, saying: "This is my blood, the new testament blood which must be shed to set all men free from their sins. Do this in memory of me.

"My dear children, I have a new commandment for you: Always love one another. Yes, love as I have loved you. There is one sign that will mark you out as my followers, for all the world to see: your enduring love for one another."

CHAPTER 53

The Way to the Father

Matthew 26:31-35; Mark 14:27-31;
Luke 22:31-34; John 13:31—14:14

The Cenacle, 8 p.m., Thursday,
April 6, 30 A.D.

Then Jesus said: "At last the Son of Man has entered the final stage of his mortal life; it will bring him to ultimate glory — very soon now. My dear children, our time together is short: you cannot come where I am going."

Simon Peter asked him: "Lord, where are you going? Why can't I follow you? I am ready to lay down my life for you."

"O Simon, dear Simon, Satan has obtained permission to shake all of you like wheat in a sieve; but I have prayed for you, Simon, that your faith may never fail. And the strength of all believers will rest on your repentant shoulders."

"Lord, even if everyone else should run away, *I* never will. I am ready to go with you to prison — even to death!"

"Believe me, Peter, this very night, before the second cockcrow, you will disown me three times over. . . .

"My dear children, there must be no more worrying, no more anxiety and fear. Have faith in me as in God himself. Even though I am going away, I am coming back again; then I will take you to myself, to my own home; there we will be together forever. . . . You know how to find your way there, don't you?"

Thomas said: "But Lord, we don't know where you're going; how can we possibly know the way?"

"I am the way," replied Jesus. "I am truth and life itself. Nobody can come to the Father except through me. If you really knew me, you would recognize my Father, too. In fact, you do know him: he is here before your eyes."

Philip broke in: "Lord, please let us see the Father; that is all we want."

"O, Philip! Have I been among you all this time without your really knowing who I am? The man who has seen me has seen the Father. Don't you believe that *I* am in the Father, and the *Father* is in me? Everything I have said and done comes from the Father who lives in me — not from myself alone."

CHAPTER 54

Jesus Promises the Holy Spirit
John 14:15-26; 15:26-27; 16:5-15; 7:37-39

The Cenacle, 8 p.m., Thursday,
April 6, 30 A.D.

"If you truly love me, you will keep my commandments; then I will ask the Father and he will
give you another Paraclete to be with you always —
the truth-giving Spirit in person. The world will not
accept him, because it cannot see him or feel his presence. But you will know him; he will stay permanent-
ly with you — within your hearts.

"Of course, I will not leave you orphans; I am
coming back to you. The man who keeps my commandments, he is the one who *really* loves me; he will
win my Father's love. I will love him, too, and reveal
myself to him."

Here Jude asked: "Lord, how is it possible for
you to make a personal appearance to us, without
other people seeing you as well?"

Jesus replied: "When a man loves me he holds
firmly to my teaching; by doing so he will win my Father's love, and we will both come to him and make
our home in his heart. I have already told you all this.
Well, the Holy Spirit will be your new teacher. He
will make everything clear and help you to remember
all I have told you. He will bear witness to what I am;
you, too, are to be my witnesses, you who have been
with me right from the beginning.

"Now I am going back to him who sent me. This makes you sad at heart. But it's for your good that I am going away; unless I depart, the Paraclete cannot come to you. And when he does come he will prove how wrong the world is not to believe in me; he will prove the justice of my claims, from my return to the Father; he will prove that sentence was really passed on the prince of this world — not on me. It is my cause he will take up; he will not speak for himself, but only to bring glory to me and to my Father.

"I still have a lot more to tell you, but you cannot possibly take it all in just now. Never mind, the Spirit of Truth will be your guide into the very depths of truth itself — absolute, entire truth."

Six months earlier, on the last day of the Feast of Tents, Jesus spoke these words in the Temple: "If any man is thirsty, let him come to me; if he has faith in me, he can quench his thirst." This is what Sacred Scripture says: "From his heart fountains of living water shall flow." Here he was speaking of the Holy Spirit, who would come to all believers after Jesus was glorified.

CHAPTER 55

Why Christians Will Be Hated
John 15:18—16:4, 16-23, 33; 14:27

**The Cenacle, 8 p.m., Thursday,
April 6, 30 A. D.**

"When the world hates you remember how violently it hated me before you. If you were worldly men, the world would accept you as its own and love you; but you don't belong there, because I have chosen you out of the world. That is why the world will hate you. They will persecute you just as they persecuted me; they will pay no more attention to your words than to mine. They will treat you like this, simply because you bear my name. If I had not come into the world, spoken to them, and worked such miracles as no one else ever did, they would not be guilty of sin; as it is they have no excuse. With eyes wide open they have hated both me *and* my Father.

"I am telling you all this so that your faith may not be shaken unexpectedly. The time is coming when people will imagine they are doing God a service by putting you to death. They will do such things because they never had any true knowledge of the Father, or of me.

"In a little while you won't be able to see me; but after another little while you will see me again."

When they heard this the apostles began to ask one another, "What's this 'little while'? We don't know what he means."

Jesus, seeing how puzzled they were, said: "Let me tell you. You will be sad and sorry men, while the world enjoys itself; you will be deeply distressed, but your sorrow will be turned into joy. A woman in childbirth feels distress when her time comes; yet as soon as she gives birth to her child she forgets her sufferings in her newfound joy. So it is with you: for the moment you are deeply distressed; but I will see you again, and then there will be joy in your hearts — a joy no one can take away from you.

"Peace is my parting gift: my own inner peace — not a worldly peace. In me alone you will find peace; in the world only distress and sorrow. But never lose heart: I have already won the battle against the world."

CHAPTER 56

Jesus' Prayer of Sacrificial Offering
John 17:1-26

The Cenacle, 9 p.m., Thursday, April 6, 30 A.D.*

When they had sung the hymn of praise, Jesus prayed with eyes raised to heaven: "Father, the hour has come to glorify your Son, so that he may give the glory back to you by bringing eternal life to all those you have entrusted to his care." (Eternal life means knowing and loving you, the only true God, and your ambassador Jesus Christ.)

"I have brought glory to you by completing the work you gave me to do on earth; now, Father, please exalt me at your side in that glory I had with you before the world began.

"I have shown the men you entrusted to my care what and who you really are. The end of my earthly life is near; but they must stay on while I return to you. I do not ask that you take them out of the world, but that you keep them from harm. They are not of the world anymore than I am of the world. Just as you sent me as your ambassador so I am sending them into the world as my ambassadors, and offering myself as a victim for them that they, too, may be completely dedicated witnesses to the truth.

*Cf. Chapter 34.

"I am not praying for them only; I am praying also for those who will believe in me through their preaching. My prayer is that they may be all united together, united in us, just as you, Father, are in me and I in you. May they all be one, as we are one: I, living in them, as you are in me. This will bring them to perfect unity and convince the world that I am truly your ambassador, loving them just as you love me.

"Father, this is my great desire: May everyone entrusted to my care on earth be with me in heaven, contemplating the glory that is mine from all eternity. Father, dear Father, I have made known and will continue to make known your will to them: so that your tremendous love for me may dwell in their hearts — and I may be there also."

Chapter 57

Anguish of Mind and Sweat of Blood

Matthew 26:30, 36-46;
Mark 14:26, 32-42; Luke 22:39-46;
John 18:1; 12:27-29

Gethsemane, 10 p.m., Thursday, April 6, 30 A.D.

When he had finished his prayer Jesus went out with his apostles across the Kedron to the foot of Olivet, where there was a garden called Gethsemane. He went in as usual, leaving his apostles at the gate. "Sit down here," he said, "while I go in there and pray."

He tore himself away from them (taking only Peter, James and John) and went about a stone's throw away into the garden. As the feeling of sadness, dread and desolation mounted up within him he said to them: "I am plunged deep in sorrow; it is breaking my heart. Won't you please stay here and keep watch with me?"

Then he went on a little farther by himself, sank to his knees, and fell prostrate on the ground, praying: "Dear Father, you can do all things; please spare me this ordeal. No, not what *I* want, only what *you* want."

He went over to the three apostles and found them asleep. He called out: "Simon, how can you

MOUNT OLIVET

sleep? Couldn't you keep watch with me even for an hour? Stay awake and keep praying, that you may not fail in the coming trial. Although the spirit is willing, human nature is weak."

Then he went away and prayed again: "O my Father, if I *must* face this ordeal, then *your* will be done."

Coming back once more he found them asleep: they just could not keep their eyes open. So he left them and gave himself to prayer a third time. And now an angel from heaven appeared visibly to him, giving him courage for the struggle against the deep distress he felt in his soul; his prayer grew to such a vehement intensity that his sweat became blood-laden, trickling to the ground in big, thick drops.

His prayer finished, he stood up and rejoined his apostles, saying to them: "It is all over now. The hour has come for the Son of Man to be betrayed into the hands of sinners. On your feet, men! We must be on our way. Look, here comes my betrayer now."

A few days earlier Jesus spoke these words in the Temple: "Oh, how my soul is in turmoil! Shall I say: 'Father, please spare me this ordeal'? No! This hour of trial is the whole purpose of my mortal life. 'Father, make known the glory of your own loving person.'"

A voice came from heaven (the bystanders thought it was thunder, or maybe an angel speaking): "I have done so, and I will again make known my love through you."

CHAPTER 58

The Betrayal and Arrest of Jesus

Matthew 26:47-56; Mark 14:43-52; Luke 22:47-53; John 18:2-12

Gethsemane, Midnight, Thursday, April 6, 30 A.D.

While the words were still on Jesus' lips, a large force of Roman soldiers (led by a captain) and Jewish police came on the scene, carrying swords and clubs, with lanterns and torches; they had been sent by the chief priests and Pharisees.

At the head of this group was Judas, one of the Twelve. Without hesitation he walked up to Jesus, saying, "Hello, Master," and kissed him ostentatiously. (This was the prearranged identification: "The one I kiss is your man; make sure you capture him.")

Jesus said to him: "O Judas, my dear friend, would you betray the Son of Man with a kiss?"

Well aware of what was going to happen to him, Jesus stepped forward to meet his captors. "Who are you looking for?" he asked.

"Jesus of Nazareth."

"*I* am Jesus of Nazareth."

When he said this to them, they pushed backward and fell to the ground in confusion. On recovering, they laid hands on Jesus and held him prisoner. In a flash Simon Peter had his sword out and swung it at Malchus, the high priest's servant, slashing off his right ear.

But Jesus intervened. "Stop! No more of this." And he touched the man's ear and healed it.

Then he spoke to Peter: "Put your sword away; all who draw the sword will perish by the sword. Don't you know I have only to ask my Father and at once he would send more than 50,000 angels to my side? But how then could the scriptures come true? Must I not submit to the ordeal destined for me by my Father himself? The forces of darkness have now taken command."

At this point his apostles, one and all, turned their backs on him and ran for their lives.

Chapter 59

Peter Disowns His Master

Matthew 26:57-58, 69-75;
Mark 14:53-54, 66-72;
Luke 22:54-62; John 18:13-27

Caiphas' House, 2 a.m., Friday, April 7, 30 A.D.

The police tied Jesus' hands and marched him off to Caiphas, who questioned him about his followers and his teaching.

Jesus answered: "I have always taught in public; I have said *nothing* in secret. These people here know my teaching; why don't you ask *them?*"

No sooner had he spoken than one of the Temple police hit him in the face. "That's no way to answer the high priest," he said.

"If I have said anything wrong," Jesus replied, "then tell me what it was; if not, why strike me like that?"

Peter and John had followed Jesus into Caiphas' palace. It was a cold night, so Peter joined a group around a brazier of coals in the open courtyard to warm himself. A servant girl came up, took a close look at him sitting there in the firelight, and said: "Weren't you with the Nazarene named Jesus?"

He denied it in front of everyone: "I have never heard of him, girl; I don't know what you're talking about."

Then as he moved to the gateway, a rooster

crowed. A few minutes later the girl at the gate noticed him and said to some men nearby: "That fellow there is one of them."

Again he denied it, this time with an oath. "No, I'm not. I've never heard of the man."

About an hour later a relative of Malchus said to him: "Didn't I see you with him in the garden?" Then all those standing there joined in: "You're one of them for sure; why, your Galilean accent gives you away."

At this Peter started to curse and swear: "I . . . am . . . not! I tell you I don't know the man."

While the words were on his lips, another rooster crowed. At that moment the Lord turned his head and looked straight at Peter. Immediately Jesus' words ("Today, before the second cockcrow, you will disown me three times over") flashed into his mind and he rushed outside, racked with sobs of bitter remorse.

CHAPTER 60

The Jewish Trial

Matthew 26:67-68; 27:1; 26:59-66;
27:3-10; Mark 14:65; 15:1; 14:55-64;
Luke 22:66-71; Acts 1:15-20

The Temple, 5 a.m., Friday,
April 7, 30 A.D.

The guards who held Jesus prisoner beat him up and spat in his face; they blindfolded him and hit him with their fists, saying as they did so: "Now, Messiah, prophesy who hit you that time!"

As soon as it was light the Jewish council brought him before their Supreme Court of Justice. They tried their utmost to find some evidence on which they could condemn him to death; but they failed completely. Though many people accused him falsely, their evidence was contradictory.

In the end two perjurors stood up and declared that they had heard him say: *(a)* "I *will* destroy this temple made by men, and within three days I will build another without human aid"; *(b)* "I *can* destroy the temple of God and rebuild it again within three days." But even on this charge their evidence did not tally in every detail.

Then the high priest himself rose to his feet and asked Jesus: "Have you nothing to say for yourself? What about all this evidence they've brought against you?"

But he remained silent, making no reply at all.

So the high priest put this formal question: "I command you by the living God to tell us under oath: Are you the Messiah?"

Then he said to them: "If I did tell you, you would never believe me; and were I to cross-question you, I know you would not tell me the truth. But this I will tell you: soon now you will see the Son of Man again, enthroned at the Almighty's right hand, coming back on the clouds of heaven."

They all said: "So you *are* the Son of God then!"

And Jesus declared: "Yes, I am."

At this the high priest tore his tunic and said: "Listen to his blasphemy! You've heard it straight from his own mouth. What is your verdict now?"

Back came their decision: "Guilty! Death!"

When Judas realized that Jesus had been condemned to death, he was seized with remorse. So he brought back their thirty pieces of silver to the chief priests and elders, with the words: "I did wrong; I betrayed an innocent man."

"What's that got to do with us?" they replied; "it's *your* problem." With that he flung the coins down on the Temple pavement and went away and hanged himself. The place of his suicide was later named Hakeldama — the Field of Blood — because it was bought with the pieces of silver, "the price of blood."

Chapter 61

The Trial Before
the Roman Governor

Matthew 27:2, 11-23; Mark 15: 1-15;
Luke 23:1-23; John 18:28-40

Antonia, 8 a.m., Friday,
April 7, 30 A.D.

Then they rose up in a body, bound his hands
again, and led him off to the governor's residence.

They would not go in, so Pilate came out to
them. "What's the charge against this man?" he
asked.

They proceeded to make the following accusa-
tions: "We found him inciting our nation to revolt,
telling the people not to pay their taxes to Caesar,
and claiming that he is the Messiah in person — in
your language, a king."

Pilate went back into the fortress and questioned
Jesus: "Well, *are* you the king of the Jews?"

"My kingdom is not a worldly one. If it were, my
own soldiers would be fighting to prevent me from
falling into the hands of the Jewish leaders. No, my
kingdom is not something earthly at all."

"So you *are* a king, then?"

"Yes, you are right; I *am* a king. I came into this
world for one purpose only: to bear witness to the
truth."

"Truth!" said Pilate. "What is truth?"

And with that he went out to face the chief priests, declaring: "This man is not guilty."

It was the custom of the governor at paschal time to release a prisoner — anyone they asked for. So, when the crowd made the usual request, Pilate answered them: "Shall I set free the king of the Jews?"

At the time there was a notorious murderer in prison, Jesus Barabbas. The chief priests worked on the mob to ask for his release instead. So, when the governor gave them the choice, "Which of the two shall I set free? Jesus Barabbas or Jesus Messiah?" a roar went up from the crowd: "No, not him! We . . . want . . . Barabbas! Put this man to death! Crucify him! Crucify him!"

"Why, what wrong has he done?" said Pilate. "I cannot find any charge against him punishable by death. I will have him flogged and then release him."

CHAPTER 62

Jesus Flogged,
Crowned and Condemned

Matthew 27:26-31, 24-25; Mark
15:15-20; Luke 23:24-25; John 19:1-16

Antonia, 10 a.m., Friday,
April 7, 30 A.D.

After the flogging the Roman guards put a scarlet
cloak on Jesus, twisted some thorn twigs into a
crown, and put it on his head — and a stick in his
right hand. They paraded before him, bowing low in
mockery, saying, "Your Royal Highness, King of the
Jews!" They jeered as they punched him in the face.
They spat on him; and taking the stick from his hand
they hit him over the head with it.

Then Pilate brought Jesus outside again, still
wearing the crown of thorns and the scarlet cloak,
and said to the crowd: "Look at who's royal!"

As soon as they caught sight of Jesus the chief
priests and their satellites shouted at the top of their
voices: "Crucify him! Crucify him! Our law says he
must die, because of his claim to be the Son of God."

When Pilate heard this he was more afraid than
ever. He took Jesus back into the fortress and asked
him: "Tell me who you really are." But Jesus made
him no answer. Pilate then said: "Why won't you
speak to me? Don't you realize it is in my power to
release or crucify you?"

Jesus answered: "You would have no power over me at all, if it had not been given you from above."

This decided Pilate; he was determined now to set him free. But the Jewish leaders shouted at him: "If you let this man go, you will be out of favor with Caesar. Any claimant to the throne is Caesar's enemy."

When Pilate heard this threat, he brought Jesus out and sat down on the judgment seat. "Well, there's your king!" he taunted.

The crowd roared: "Death! Death! Crucify him!"

"What!" Pilate jeered. "Am I to crucify your king?"

The chief priests answered: "We have no king but Caesar."

So Pilate, sensing he would have a riot on his hands at any moment, sent for water and washed his hands in full view of the crowd, declaring: "I take no responsibility for the death of this man; it's entirely *your* doing."

With one voice they all replied: "His blood be upon *us,* and upon our children."

CHAPTER 63

The Crucifixion of Jesus

Matthew 27:31-38; Mark 15:20-28;
Luke 23:26-34, 38; John 19:16-27

**Calvary, Noon, Friday,
April 7, 30 A.D.**

The Roman guards marched Jesus off to be crucified. At first he carried the cross himself, but along
the way they forced a spectator, Simon of Cyrene, to
carry it for him.

A huge crowd followed him, including some
women who beat their breasts and mourned over
him. Jesus stopped and spoke to them: "Please don't
shed your tears for me, daughters of Jerusalem; you
should be weeping for yourselves and for your children.

"Mark my words: a time is surely coming when
people will say, 'Fortunate indeed are the childless
women!' Everyone will be calling out to the moun-
tains: 'Fall on us! Bury us!' Yes, if this is what hap-
pens to the green wood, what will be the fate of the
dry?"

When they reached Calvary (in Hebrew, Golgotha) the women offered him drugged wine; he took
a sip but would not drink it.

It was not yet noon when they nailed him to the
cross — between two criminals. All the time Jesus
kept saying over and over: "Father, forgive them;
they don't realize what they are doing."

147

Over his head they fixed a placard specifying the charge against him: "Jesus of Nazareth, King of the Jews."

When the chief priests read this they went straight to Pilate and demanded that he change the title to "This man *claimed* to be a king."

Pilate retorted: "I have written and it *stays* written."

The soldiers divided his clothes among them, a quarter share each. Only his seamless robe was left. "Better not cut it up," they said, "we'll toss for it." By doing so this text of Sacred Scripture came true: "They divided my clothes among them; they cast lots for my robe."

Meanwhile there were others standing near Jesus' cross: his mother, with her sister-in-law Mary, wife of Cleophas, and Mary Magdalen. As soon as Jesus noticed his mother at his side, and that apostle who was his best friend with her, he said to her: "Woman of Destiny,* take him for your son." Then he said to John: "She will be a mother to you." And from then onward John cared for her, taking her to live in his own home.

*Simply "Woman" in the original; this does not indicate disrespect to Mary: it is a title of honor (see Chapter 12).

(FACING PAGE)
JESUS ON HIS WAY TO CALVARY

CHAPTER 64

The Death of Jesus

Matthew 27:39-56; Mark 15:29-41;
Luke 23:35-49; John 19:25-30

Calvary, 3 p.m., Friday,
April 7, 30 A.D.

A crowd of people stood and stared, gloating and jeering at him: "Hey, you! Why don't you rescue yourself?"

The officials were there, too, making insulting remarks: "If he is God's chosen Messiah, why doesn't he step down from the cross here and now? If we see him do that, then we'll believe."

Even one of the criminals hanging there with him joined in: "If you're really the Messiah, why don't you rescue yourself — and us, too?"

But the other rebuked him: "Is this the time to offend God, seeing you're undergoing the same sentence yourself? We're only getting what we deserve; but this man never did anything wrong in his whole life. . . . Jesus, please remember me when you come back in glory to take possession of your kingdom."

He replied: "I solemnly promise you, this very day you shall be with me in paradise."

From noon until three in the afternoon there was darkness over the whole countryside — the sun was blacked out. About three o'clock Jesus uttered a loud cry: "My God, my God, why have you forsaken me?"

Then he said: "I'm thirsty." One of the soldiers

quickly ran for a sponge, soaked it in wine, fixed it on a spear, and put it to Jesus' lips. He drank the wine and spoke out loud in a strong voice: "My task is completed. Father, I willingly put myself in your loving hands."

Then he bowed his head and gave up his spirit.

At that moment there was a violent earthquake: the sanctuary curtain of the Temple was torn from top to bottom, and rock tombs were split wide open. When the centurion on guard saw how Jesus died he testified: "This man was *truly* God's Son." And the crowds who had watched all this went home beating their breasts.

CHAPTER 65

The Burial of Jesus

Matthew 27:57-61; Mark 15:42-47;
Luke 23:50-56; John 19:31-42

**Calvary, 6 p.m., Friday,
April 7, 30 A.D.**

After it was all over, a wealthy and distinguished councilor, Joseph of Arimathea (a good, honest man, who had not agreed with the council's condemnation of Jesus), courageously went to Pilate and asked for Jesus' body.

Pilate, astonished at such a speedy death, sent for the centurion on guard and asked him if Jesus was dead already. On hearing the centurion's report, he gave orders for the corpse to be handed over to Joseph.

The Jewish officials had already asked Pilate to have the men's legs broken and their bodies removed (their law forbade crucified persons to remain on the cross over the sabbath). So a new detachment of soldiers came and broke the legs of both those crucified with Jesus; but seeing that Jesus was already dead they did not break his legs. (This was just as the scriptures foretold: "Not a single bone of his shall be broken.") One of them thrust a spear into his side, and immediately blood and water flowed out.

Joseph returned with Nicodemus (the man who had once visited Jesus under cover of darkness) carrying about 100 pounds of powdered myrrh and aloes.

JESUS' BODY IS TAKEN DOWN FROM THE CROSS

They took Jesus' body down from the cross, wrapped it in a clean linen shroud along with the spices (this is a Jewish burial custom), and laid it to rest in a nearby grave cut out of the solid rock, rolling a large stone across the doorway. (This vault had been prepared by Joseph for himself in a garden near the place where Jesus had been crucified. It was quite new — no one had ever been buried in it.)

Mary Magdalen, Mary Cleophas and Salome Zebedee, along with other women who had come with Jesus from Galilee, followed the burial party; they noted carefully the position of the tomb and how his body had been laid to rest.

The sabbath lights were just then beginning to shine.

Note: For the account of Nicodemus' visit to Jesus, see John 3:1-15.

CHAPTER 66

The Empty Tomb

Matthew 28:1-10; Mark 16:1-11;
Luke 24:1-12; John 20:1-18

**Alongside Calvary, Sunday Morning,
April 9, 30 A.D.**

Early on Sunday morning, while it was still dark,
the women set out with aromatic spices to embalm
Jesus' body, arriving at the tomb just at sunrise. The
first thing they saw was the large stone already rolled
back from the door of the tomb (an angel had come
down from heaven and rolled it away).

They went in, but searched in vain for the body
of the Lord Jesus. At once Mary Magdalen rushed
off to tell Peter and John: "The Lord is gone from his
tomb! Someone must have stolen the body!"

Peter and John came running as fast as they
could. They entered the tomb and saw the shroud
lying there undisturbed; but the chinband was a little
apart by itself, neatly rolled up.

Puzzling over this they went off, leaving Mary
still standing by the tomb crying her eyes out. She
peered into the tomb and saw two angels sitting on
the bench where Jesus' body had lain — one at the
head, one at the feet. They asked her why she was crying.

"Because somebody has stolen my Lord, and I
don't know what has become of him." As she said

this she turned around and saw Jesus standing there, but she did not recognize him.

He asked her: "My poor girl, why are you crying? Are you looking for someone?"

Taking him for the gardener she said: "Sir, if you're the one that carried him away, please tell me where you have put him, and I'll go and get him."

Jesus said to her: "Mary!"

At once she recognized him. "Oh, Master!"

Then Jesus said: "You don't have to hold onto me: I'm not leaving you to go back to the Father for some time yet. . . . Run off now to my little family with the good news."

So she went and announced to his grief-stricken followers: "I've seen the Lord!"

But they did not believe her.

(FACING PAGE)
LORENZO FERRI'S
"IMAGE OF JESUS' FACE FROM THE SACRED SHROUD"

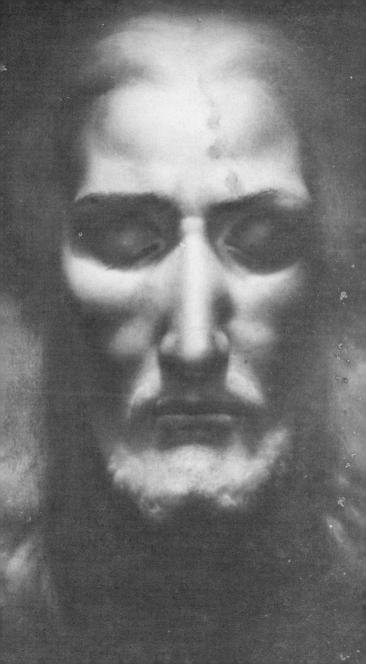

CHAPTER 67

A Walk to Remember
Mark 16:13; Luke 24:13-35
Emmaus, Sunday Afternoon, April 9, 30 A.D.

That same day two of his followers were walking to Emmaus, a village seven miles from Jerusalem, discussing all that had happened. While they were so engrossed, Jesus himself came up and joined them; but he looked different, and they didn't recognize him.

He asked them: "What are you arguing about? And why such long faces?"

They stopped in amazement: "What!" exclaimed the one called Cleophas. "You must be the only pilgrim in Jerusalem that has not heard what has just happened there."

"Well, what did happen?"

"Why, all about Jesus of Nazareth, truly a great prophet both in the eyes of God and the people. Haven't you heard how our rulers handed him over to be put to death on the cross? And we had hoped he was the one destined to set Israel free. . . . That was three days ago. True, some of our women at his tomb early this morning said they had seen angels who told them he was alive. So some of the men went there to investigate; but they didn't see him."

"How dense you are! How slow to believe! Did not the prophets of old foretell that the Messiah had first to suffer, and only then begin his glorious reign?"

And beginning with Moses he explained to them everything the scriptures had to say about himself.

By now they were approaching their destination. When he pretended to be going farther on, they insisted: "You must stay the night with us; it's almost dark already."

So he went into their house and sat down for the evening meal. He picked up a loaf of bread, said grace, broke it into pieces, and handed it to them. In a flash their eyes were opened and they recognized him. . . . But he vanished as they stared.

Then both of them spoke: "Didn't he warm our cold hearts and set them on fire with joy when he made the scriptures so clear to us as we walked along the road?"

They got to their feet at once and hurried back to Jerusalem to find a group of his followers talking excitedly and saying: "It's true! The Lord has risen! Simon saw him!"

CHAPTER 68

"The Mark of the Nails"

Luke 24:36-43; John 20:19-29

The Cenacle, Sunday Evening, April 9, 30 A.D.

It was now evening of the same day; the apostles were sitting around a table in the room where they had met, with the doors bolted for fear of the Jewish officials. While they were actually discussing the appearance of Jesus, he came in person and stood there among them, with the greeting: "Peace be in your hearts."

They shrank back, frightened out of their wits, thinking they were seeing a ghost.

"Why are you so terrified?" he said to them. "Come here and look at my hands and feet — it's really me! Go on, touch me and see for yourselves; a ghost hasn't flesh and bones as I have." (While he was speaking he showed them his hands, his feet and his side, too.)

But they were so dazed with joy and wonder that they could hardly believe it was true. So he asked them: "Have you anything here to eat?" When they brought him a piece of grilled fish, he picked it up and ate it and a honeycomb as well, before their eyes.

Thomas, one of the apostles, was absent when the Lord came. The others kept on telling him: "It's true! We *did* see the Lord."

But all he said was: "Until I've seen with my own

160

eyes the mark of the nails in his hands . . . until I've put my finger into the nail holes . . . and my hand into his side, you'll never make me believe."

A week later the apostles were in the same room; and this time Thomas was with them. Jesus came again through closed and bolted doors and stood there among them. "Peace be in your hearts," he said. He turned to Thomas. "Come here and feel my hands with your finger. Let me have your hand; put it into my side. Don't doubt anymore — just believe."

Thomas answered: "My Lord and my God!"

Jesus said to him: "You now believe because you have seen me. To believe without seeing — that's best of all."

CHAPTER 69

A Miraculous Catch of Fish
John 21:1-12
Tabgha, April, 30 A.D.

The next time Jesus appeared to his followers was by the lake. It happened like this: Peter said, "I'm going fishing."

"We'll come along, too," said Thomas, Nathanael and the two sons of Zebedee.

So the five of them went out on the lake in a boat; but they didn't catch a single fish all night.

At daybreak Jesus was standing on the shore — though they had no idea who he was.

He called out: "Caught anything yet, friends? . . . Well, cast the net to starboard and you'll get a haul."

So they let out the net and caught such a shoal of fish they were unable to pull it in. It was then the disciple whom Jesus loved whispered to Peter: "It's the Lord!"

At these words Peter put on his robe and jumped into the water, leaving the others to tow the catch ashore — they were only about 100 yards out.

When they landed, a fire was already burning, with fish grilling on it — and loaves of bread ready to be eaten.

When Jesus asked them to bring some of their catch, Peter went and had the net hauled onto the beach. It was loaded with fish (153 of them — all big ones!); and even with all that number, the net wasn't torn.

Then Jesus called to them: "Come along now and have breakfast." And he himself waited on them, passing around the bread, and the fish as well. . . . None of them could summon up the courage to ask him who he was — they knew in their hearts that it was the Lord.*

*For the sequel to this scene, see Chapter 41.

CHAPTER 70

The Ascension of Our Lord
Mark 16:19-20; Luke 24:44-53;
Acts 1:3-15

Mount Olivet, Thursday,
May 18, 30 A.D.

He appeared to them many other times over a period of forty days, instructing them about the kingdom of God.

He told them: "Remember all I taught you while I still walked the roads with you; how everything written of me in the Law of Moses, in the Prophets, and in the Psalms must be fulfilled."

Then he enlightened their minds so that they were enabled to understand the scriptures.

At last the day came when he was to be taken up into heaven. As he led them out along the Bethany road, they asked him: "Lord, are you going to set up the kingdom today?"

He replied: "The Father himself has fixed the day and the hour; it is no concern of yours. All you have to do is wait for the Holy Spirit to come down upon you; you will receive power from him to bear witness to me in Jerusalem, throughout Judea and Samaria — even to the ends of the earth."

When Jesus had said this he gave them his blessing; while he was in the act of blessing them he was lifted up in the air, mounting higher and higher until he disappeared in a cloud.

JOSEPH KUNDRAT'S "ASCENSION OF OUR LORD"

As they strained their eyes to watch his ascension, suddenly two men in dazzling white stood there beside them, with the message: "This same Jesus will come back again one day, in exactly the same way as you've just watched him going up to heaven."

Then they bowed down to worship him enthroned now at God's right hand, and with joyful hearts went back to the upstairs room in Jerusalem, where they gave their whole time to prayer — with Jesus' mother, Mary.

CHAPTER 71

The Coming of the Holy Spirit
Acts 2:1-36
The Cenacle, Sunday, May 28, 30 A.D.

They were all gathered together in the same room, early in the morning of Pentecost Day. Suddenly a loud roar (like a violent windstorm) came from heaven, penetrating the whole house. Then they saw tongues (just like fiery flames) dividing up and coming to rest on each person's head. The Holy Spirit himself took complete possession of them, so that they started to talk in foreign languages — using the exact words he put into their mouths.

Attracted by the noise, a large crowd (including men from every country of the world) soon gathered. Startled and astonished, they could hardly believe their own ears: "Aren't all these men Galileans? How is it that each of us hears them proclaiming God's wonders in his own mother tongue? What's it all about? . . . They must have been drinking too much wine!"

Then Peter came forward as the spokesman for the apostolic group and addressed them: "Fellow Jews, these people are not drunk at all; why, they haven't yet broken their fast this morning. No, this is what the prophet Joel said would happen: 'In messianic times, God says, I will pour my Spirit on all mankind — men and women alike.'

"Men of Israel, listen to this: Jesus of Nazareth

proved himself a man sent by God (there is no need to recall the miracles he did among you). This is the man you put to death; but God has raised him up from the dead — we are all witnesses of it. It is of him that David spoke: 'My whole being is full of confidence that you will not leave my soul in the abode of the dead, or allow the body of your faithful servant to rot in the grave.'

"Exalted now at God's right hand, he has carried out his promise to send the Holy Spirit — as you've just seen and heard for yourselves. So all Jewry must acknowledge as certain and true: This Jesus whom you crucified is both your Lord *and* your Messiah."

CHAPTER 72

A New Community

Acts 2:37-47

The Temple, Sunday, May 28, 30 A.D.

When they heard this, their consciences were stung; and they asked Peter and his fellow apostles, "Brethren, what must we do?"

"Repent," Peter said to them, "and be baptized, every one of you, in the name of Jesus Christ, to have your sins forgiven; then you will receive the gift of the Holy Spirit. This promise is for you and for your children, and for all those, however far away, whom the Lord our God calls to himself."

So all those who had taken his words to heart were baptized, and about 3,000 souls were won for the Lord that day. These occupied themselves continually with the apostles' teaching and fellowship, and the breaking of bread, and the fixed times of prayer, and every soul was struck with awe, so many were the wonders and signs performed by the apostles in Jerusalem. They persevered with one accord, day by day, in the Temple worship, and, as they broke bread in this house or that, took their share of food with gladness and simplicity of heart, praising God, and winning favor with all the people. And each day the Lord added to their fellowship others that were to be saved.

And they went out and preached everywhere, the Lord aiding them, and attesting his word by miracles.

Index

— A —

Abraham — 31, 62, 108ff
Adultery — 51
Advocate — See Paraclete
Agony in garden — 134ff
Ain Karim — 18
Almighty — 18, 142
Ambassador, Jesus sent as — 83, 97, 109, 132ff
Ambassadors, apostles sent as — 83ff, 97, 132ff
　　See also Mission of apostles
Andrew — 35, 42, 74, 86
Angel(s) — 33ff, 36, 106, 136, 138, 155, 158
　　Appears to Zachary — 13ff
　　Appears to Mary — 15ff
　　Appears to Joseph — 20, 26
　　Appear to shepherds — 21ff
　　Appear to Jesus — 34, 136
Anger — 57
　　Of Jesus — 103ff
Anna — 24
Annas — 31
Annunciation — 15ff
Antonia — 143, 145
Anxiety — 76, 126
Apostles — 35ff, 42, 68, 74ff, 80-84, 87, 90-92, 93, 97ff, 116, 122-38, 160-69
　　See also Followers
Appearances of Jesus — 97, 160-64
Arrest of Jesus — 137ff
　　Attempts at — 111, 115, 120, 122ff
Ascension of Jesus — 164ff
Augustus — See Caesar Augustus
Authority of Jesus — 39, 98, 103
　　Of Peter — 92
　　See also Prophet

— B —

Baptism — 31, 98, 169
　　Of Jesus — 31ff
Barabbas — 144
Bartholomew — See Nathanael
Beatitudes — 49
Benedictus canticle — 19
Bethany — 35, 53, 55, 78, 95, 114ff, 116, 118
　　Bethany road — 164
Bethlehem — 21ff, 25ff
Bethsaida — 84ff, 87, 91
Betrayal of Jesus — 122, 124, 136, 137
　　Foretold — 82, 90, 116

Bezatha pool — 106

Birth of Jesus — 21ff

Blasphemy, Jesus accused of — 43ff, 111, 142

Blessed Virgin — *See* Mary, Mother of Jesus

Blood of Christ — 89, 125

Body of Christ — 89, 125

Bread and fish — 84ff, 163

Bread at Last Supper — 125
Breaking of, at Emmaus — 159; at Jerusalem — 169
Of Life — 89ff

Bridegroom and wedding guests, parable of — 45ff

Burial of Jesus — 152ff

— C —

Caesar Augustus — 21

Caesar — *See* Tiberius Caesar

Caesarea Philippi — 91

Caiphas — 31, 115, 139, 141ff

Calming of storm on lake — 68

Calvary — 147ff, 150-54

Cana, wedding at — 37ff

Capharnaum — 39, 43, 47, 61, 71, 87, 89

Catch of fish, miracle of — 41, 162

Cenacle — 80-83, 97, 122-33, 160ff, 166, 167
See also Inn

Census — 21

Centurion, cure of servant — 61ff
At cross — 151, 152

Charity — 52, 57

Chief priests — 105ff, 115, 116, 137, 142, 143ff, 149
Attempt to arrest Jesus — 115, 119, 122ff
Call for Jesus' death — 145ff
See also Leaders of Jews

Church — 66ff, 169
Founding of — 92, 98, 167ff
Promise of Jesus to be with — 98

Circumcision of John the Baptist — 18
Of Jesus — 23n

Cleansing of Temple — 103

Cleophas — 45, 74, 158
See also Mary Cleophas

Cloud — 15n, 32, 94, 142, 164

Cockcrow — 126, 140

Coin of tribute — 120

Coming of Jesus — 13, 109, 114
Second coming — 55, 126ff, 128, 130ff

Commandment(s) — 80, 98, 125, 128

Commission to apostles — 74ff, 98
    See also Ambassadors; Mission of apostles

Community — 169

Condemnation of Jesus — 142, 146

Confession of faith by Peter — *See* Peter, Profession of faith

Council, Jewish — 115, 141, 152

Criminals crucified with Jesus — 147, 150

Cripple at pool — 106

Cross — 93, 147-54

Crowning with thorns — 145

Crucifixion of Jesus — 147-51

Cures — *See* Miracles

— D —

David — 15, 19, 20, 21, 47

Death of Jesus — 150ff
    Foretold — 93, 96, 103, 116
    Leaders attempt — 109, 110ff
    Leaders plot — 48, 105, 106, 111, 115, 119, 122

Decree of Emperor Augustus — 21

Dedication feast — 110

Den of thieves — 103

Denarius — 84n, 120

Denial by Peter — 139ff

Deposition of Jesus from cross — 154

Desert — 33

Devil — *See* Satan

Dinar — 84
    See also Denarius

Disciples — *See* Apostles; Followers

Doctors of the law — 27, 39, 43

Donkey (colt), Jesus rides — 116ff

Dove(s) — 24, 32, 75

Draft of fish, miracle of — 41, 162

Dragnet, parable of — 66

— E —

Ears of wheat — 47

Egypt — 26

Elders — 61, 142
    See also Leaders of Jews

Elijah — 91, 93ff

Elizabeth — 13ff, 16, 18ff

Emmanuel — 20

Emmaus — 158ff

Enemies, love of — 52

172

Entrusting of flock to Peter — 92, 97ff

Ephrem — 115

Equality of Jesus with God — *See* Father: Equality of Jesus with

Exodus — 15n

Exorcism performed by Jesus — 40, 48, 69ff
    Apostles to perform — 74
    See also Satan

Expulsion of Temple traffickers — 103

— F —

Faith — 61ff, 68, 71, 77, 83, 89, 129, 130, 161
    Peter's faith — 88, 90, 92, 126

Farmers, parable of murderous — 118ff

Fast of Jesus — 33ff

Fasting — 24, 45, 46, 58

Father — 37, 50, 52, 57ff, 74ff, 76, 80ff, 90, 92, 96, 97, 98, 128ff, 130, 138, 156, 164
    Jesus' prayer to — 82ff, 132ff, 134ff, 147
    Equality of Jesus with — 106ff, 108ff, 110ff, 127
    Father's house — 27, 57, 103

Father — *continued*
    Voice of Father — 32, 94, 136
    See also Son; Spirit

Feedbox — 21ff

Fellowship — 169

Fish, miraculous catch of — 41, 162
    Multiplication of — 84ff

Fishers of men — 41ff

Flesh — 89, 125

Flight into Egypt — 26

Flogging of Jesus — 145

Followers of Jesus — 35ff, 38, 47, 48, 49, 59, 63, 67, 74, 76ff, 90, 115, 117, 125, 139, 156, 159, 162
    Of apostles — 169
    Of John the Baptist — 31, 35, 45

Food, Jesus as — 89

Forgiveness of sin — *See* Sin, forgiveness of

Founding of Church — *See* Church: Founding of

— G —

Gabriel appears to Mary — 15ff
    Appears to Zachary — 13ff

Galilee — 31, 37ff, 43, 84, 87, 97ff, 154
    See also Lake Galilee

173

Garments of Jesus at Calvary — 149
Genesareth — *See* Lake Galilee
Gerasa — 69
Gethsemane — 134-38
Glory — 55, 93ff, 109, 129, 132, 133, 136
God and mammon, parable of — 76ff
Golden rule — 51ff
Golgotha — *See* Calvary
Good news — 40, 49
Good Samaritan, parable of — 53ff
Good shepherd, parable of — 95ff
Gospel, preach — 74, 98, 169

— H —

Hakeldama — 142
Hatred for Christians — 75, 83, 130ff
Healing miracles — *See* Miracles
Heal the sick — 74
Hermon — 93
Herod — 13, 25ff, 31
High priest — *See* Annas; Caiphas
Holiness — 57ff
Holy Spirit — *See* Spirit
Homage of Wise Men — 25ff

Horns of Hattin — 74
House built on rock, parable of — 58
Humility — 59ff, 122ff
Hypocrisy of Pharisees — 31, 120ff

— I —

Inn — 21n, 54
    See also Cenacle
Innocents, massacre of — 26
Instructions to apostles — 74ff, 116
    See also Commission to apostles
Isaac — 62
Isaiah — 39, 48, 67

— J —

Jacob — 15, 62
Jairus — 71
James (son of Zebedee) — 42, 74, 93, 134ff, 162
James (son of Cleophas) — 74
Jeremiah — 91
Jericho — 53
Jerusalem — 24, 25, 27, 33, 43, 53, 93, 97, 103, 106, 108, 110, 116, 158ff, 164-67, 169

Jerusalem — *continued*

  Destruction foretold — 117, 121

Jesus, name of — 15, 20, 23n

Jesus of Nazareth — 36, 39, 137, 149, 158, 167ff

  See also King; Son

Joel — 167

John — 35n, 42, 74, 93, 124, 134ff, 139, 149, 155, 162

John the Baptist — 31ff, 35, 91

  Disciples of — 31, 35, 45

  Name of — 13, 18

Jordan river — 31, 33, 35

Jordan valley — 59, 112

Joseph — 15, 20

  Angel appears to — 20ff, 26

  Espousal of — 20

  Goes to Bethlehem — 21ff

  Flees to Egypt — 26

  Presents Jesus — 24ff

  Returns to Nazareth from Egypt — 26

  Seeks Jesus in Jerusalem — 27

  Travels home to Nazareth — 27

Joseph of Arimathea — 152ff

Joy — 109, 131

Judas Iscariot — 74, 82, 90, 122, 124, 136, 137, 142

  See also Betrayal

Jude — 74, 128

Judea — 25, 31, 43, 110

Judgment, Day of — 55ff, 75, 114

  See also Coming of Jesus: Second coming

— K —

Kedron — 134

  See also Bethany road

Kepha — 35, 92

Keys of kingdom — 92

King — 87, 116ff, 143, 145ff, 149

  Of Israel — 15, 36

  Of the Jews — 25, 143ff, 149

Kingdom of God — 31, 40, 49, 55ff, 58, 62, 66ff, 76, 77, 78, 84, 92, 116ff, 119, 143

  Foretold by Gabriel — 15

— L —

Lake Galilee — 41, 45, 63, 66, 68, 69, 87ff, 97, 162

  See also Galilee

Lamb of God — 35

175

Lambs — 97
    See also Sheep
Lamp on stand, parable of
    — 50
Last Day — *See* Judgment,
    Day of
Last Supper — 122-33
Law of Moses — 24, 47,
    51ff, 53, 120, 152, 164
        New law of Christ —
        51ff
Lawyers — 43, 45, 47, 105,
    116, 120ff
    See also Doctors of the
        law; Leaders of Jews;
        Pharisees
Lazarus — 114ff
Leaders of Jews (officials)
    — 93, 103-11, 115, 122,
    146, 150, 152, 160
        Attempt to arrest Jesus
        — 111, 115, 119, 122
        Attempt to stone Jesus
        — 109, 110ff
        Call for Jesus' death —
        145ff
        Plot Jesus' death — 48,
        105, 106, 115, 120,
        122
        Summon council meet-
        ing — 115
        See also Chief priests;
            Elders;   Lawyers;
            Pharisees
Leaven, parable of — 67
Legion of devils — 69ff

Life — 53, 80ff, 89ff, 95,
    107, 108, 110, 114, 127,
    132
        See also Truth; Way,
            Jesus as
Light of the world — 50,
    108
Loaves — 33, 47
    See also Bread and fish
Love — 52-54, 80ff, 83,
    97ff, 107, 125, 128ff, 133,
    136

— M —

Magi — 25ff
Magnificat canticle — 18
Malchus — 138, 140
Mammon — 76ff, 103
Manger — 21ff
Martha — 114
Mary of Bethany — 114
Mary Cleophas — 149, 154
Mary Magdalen — 149,
    154, 155
Mary, Mother of Jesus
    Archangel Gabriel sent
        to — 15ff
    At cousin Elizabeth's
        — 18
    Gives birth to Jesus —
        21ff
    Marries Joseph — 20
    Presents Jesus in Tem-
        ple — 24
    Receives Wise Men —
        25

Mary — *continued*

  Returns to Nazareth
    from Egypt — 26
  Seeks Jesus in Jerusa-
    lem — 27
  At wedding of Cana —
    37
  At foot of cross — 149
  With apostles — 166

Massacre of Innocents —
  26

Master — 47, 114, 123, 156

Matthew — 45, 74

Messiah — 21, 24, 25, 32,
  35, 90, 92, 108, 110, 114,
  141, 142, 143, 144, 150,
  158, 167ff

Miracles of Jesus
  Cure of blind man —
    91
  Cure of centurion's ser-
    vant — 61ff
  Cure of cripple at pool
    — 106
  Cure of Jairus' daugh-
    ter — 71ff
  Cure of man with with-
    ered hand — 47ff
  Cure of paralytic —
    43ff
  Cure of Peter's mother-
    in-law — 39
  Cure of sick and pos-
    sessed — 40, 48, 70

Miracles — *continued*

  Cure of sick and suffer-
    ing — 49, 84
  Cure of woman with
    hemorrhage — 71
  Draft of fish — 41, 162
  Calming of storm — 68
  Multiplication of bread
    and fish — 84ff
  Raising of Lazarus —
    114ff
  Walking on water —
    87ff
  Water changed into
    wine — 37ff

Miracles of apostles — 169
  See also Mission of
    apostles

Mission of apostles — 74ff,
  84, 97ff
  See also Ambassadors

Money — *See* Mammon

Money changers driven
  from Temple — 103

Mosaic Law — *See* Law of
  Moses

Moses — 36, 93ff, 159, 164
  See also Law of Moses

Most High — 15

Mountain — 34, 93

Mount of Beatitudes — 49-
  52, 57ff

Multiplication of bread and
  fish — 84ff

Murder — 51

Murderous sharecroppers, parable of — 118ff

Mustard seed, parable of — 66ff

Mystical Body — 55ff

— N —

Nathanael (Bartholomew) — 36, 74, 162

Nazareth — 15, 20, 21, 26, 27, 31, 36, 149

Neighbor, love of — 52-54

Net, parable of — 66

New patch on old coat, parable of — 46

New wine in old wineskins, parable of — 46

Nicodemus — 153, 154n

— O —

Obedience of Jesus — 27

Officials, Jewish — *See* Leaders of Jews

Olivet, Mount — 116, 134, 164

Our Father — 57ff

Outcasts — 112

— P —

Palm branches — 116ff

Parables

Bridegroom and wedding guests — 45ff

Dragnet — 66

God and mammon — 76ff

Good Samaritan — 53ff

Good shepherd — 95ff

House built on a rock — 58

Lamp on stand — 50

Leaven — 67

Murderous sharecroppers (vinedressers) — 118ff

Mustard seed — 66ff

New patch on old coat — 46

New wine in old wineskins — 46

Pearl — 67

Pharisee and tax collector — 59ff

Prodigal son — 112ff

Rich fool — 77

Sower — 63ff

Talents (unprofitable servant) — 78ff

Treasure — 67

Unjust judge — 59

Weeds (tares) — 66

Paraclete (Advocate) — 128ff, 167

Paralytic, miraculous cure of — 43ff

Paschal feast — *See* Passover

Passover — 27, 116ff, 122ff, 144

Peace — 131

Pearl, parable of — 67

Pentecost — 167ff

Persecution — 130

Perseverance — 59

Peter (Simon) — 41ff, 74, 90, 91ff, 93, 124, 155, 159, 162, 167

    And brother Andrew — 35, 42, 74

    Denies Jesus — 139ff

    In Gethsemane — 134ff, 137ff

    Love for Jesus — 97ff, 126

    And mother-in-law — 39

    Preaches — 167ff

    Primacy of — 92, 97ff

    Profession of faith — 91ff, 126

    Protests washing of feet — 123

    Walks on water — 87ff

Pharisee and tax collector, parable of — 59ff

Pharisees — 31, 32, 43, 45, 47ff, 91, 95, 112, 117, 137

    Accuse Jesus of blasphemy — 43ff

    Attempt to arrest Jesus — 119

Pharisees — *continued*

    Hypocrisy of — 31, 120ff

    Plot Jesus' capture — 120

    See also Chief priests; Lawyers; Leaders; Sadducees

Philip — 36, 74, 84, 127

Piercing of Jesus' side — 152

Pilate — 31, 120, 143-46, 149, 152

Plain of Sharon — 76

Pontius Pilate — *See* Pilate

Possession, diabolical — *See* Exorcism

Prayer — 24, 57ff, 59ff, 169

    Of Jesus — 32, 40, 74, 82ff, 87, 91, 93, 132ff, 134ff, 147, 150ff

    See also Psalms

Preaching of apostles — 73, 83, 98, 130, 133, 169

Precedence among apostles — 122ff

Presentation of Jesus — 24ff

Primacy of Peter — 92, 97ff

Prodigal son, parable of — 112ff

Profession of faith by Peter — 91ff, 126

Promise of Jesus to give self as food — 89ff
    To be with Church — 98
Prophecy — 19, 20, 24, 39, 48, 67, 82, 103ff, 116, 149, 152, 167ff
    See also Kingdom of God; Scripture
Prophet(s) — 36, 91, 109, 116, 158ff, 164
    Jesus as — 86, 119, 158
    See also Elijah; Isaiah; Jeremiah; Joel; Moses
Providence of God — 74ff, 76ff
Psalms — 164
    See also Benedictus; Magnificat; Prayer; Simeon, Canticle of
Publicans — *See* Tax collectors

— R —

Racketeers driven from Temple — 103
Raising of Jairus' daughter, of Lazarus — *See* Resurrection
Rest — 84
Resurrection of body — 114
    Of Jesus foretold — 93, 96, 103ff, 116

Resurrection — *continued*

    Of Jairus' daughter — 71ff
    Of Jesus — 155ff
    Jesus as — 114
    Of Lazarus — 114ff
Retaliation — 51
Rich fool, parable of — 77

— S —

Sabbath — 39, 47ff, 106, 152, 154
Sadducees — 31
    See also Leaders
Salome Zebedee — 154
Salvation foretold by Zachary — 19
    Foretold by Simeon — 24
Sanhedrin — *See* Council
Satan (devil) — 33ff, 90, 92, 124, 126
    Prince of this world — 129
    Forces of Darkness — 138
Savior — 18, 19, 20, 24
Scourging of Jesus — 145
Scripture — 25, 33ff, 82, 103ff, 107, 129, 138, 149, 152, 159, 164
Self-denial — 93
Sepulcher of Jesus — 155

Serpent — 31, 75, 121
Sharecroppers, parable of murderous — 118ff
Sheep — 75ff, 84, 95ff, 98, 110
Shekel — 122
Pieces of silver — 142
See also Denarius
Shekinah, 15n
See also Cloud
Shepherds — 21ff
Shepherd, good — 95ff
Of Israel — 25
See also Sheep
Shroud of Jesus — 154
Sign of contradiction — 24
Simeon, Canticle of — 24
Simon Peter — *See* Peter
Simon of Cyrene — 147
Simon the Patriot — 74
Sin, forgiveness of — 19, 31, 43ff, 97, 169
Sinners — *See* Tax collectors
Snake — 31, 75, 121
Solomon — 76
Solomon's Cloister — 110
Son — 32, 94, 98, 106ff, 109, 132
Firstborn — 21
Of David — 15, 19, 117
Of God — 16, 32, 36, 88, 92, 111, 114, 142, 145, 151
Of Joseph — 36

Son — *continued*
Of Man — 36, 44, 47, 55, 89, 91, 93, 116, 123, 126, 136, 137, 142
Of the Most High — 15, 69
See also Father; Messiah; Spirit
Sower, parable of — 63ff
Spirit — 13, 15, 18, 19, 24, 32, 75, 97, 98, 128ff, 167, 169
Coming of — 167ff
Power of conceiving — 15ff, 20
Star of Bethlehem — 25
Storm on lake — 68
Supreme Court of Justice — 141
Sword of sorrow — 24

— T —

Tabgha — 45, 162
Talents, parable of — 78ff
Talion, law of — 51
Tares, parable of — 66
Taxes — 120, 143
Tax collectors — 45, 112
See also Pharisee and tax collector, parable of; Taxes
Teachers — *See* Doctors of the law

181

Teaching of Jesus — 39ff, 41, 49, 63, 108ff, 110, 118, 127, 128, 139
    Of apostles — 83, 130, 133, 169
    See also Gospel, preach; Parables
Temple — 13, 24, 27, 33, 103ff, 141ff, 151, 169
    Jesus found in — 27
    Jesus teaches in — 106ff, 108ff, 110ff, 118ff, 120, 129, 136
    Racketeers driven from — 103
Temptation of Jesus — 33ff
Tents, feast of — 108, 129
Thieves crucified with Jesus — 147, 150
Thomas — 74, 127, 160ff, 162
Tiberius Caesar — 31, 120, 143, 146
Tomb of Jesus — 155
Transfiguration of Christ — 93ff
Trials of Jesus — 141-46
Tribute — *See* Taxes
Treasure, parable of — 67
Trust — 74ff, 76ff
Truth — 83, 108, 127, 129, 143
    See also Life; Way, Jesus as
Twelve — *See* Apostles

— U —

Unity of faithful — 83, 96
    Of Father and Son — 83, 110ff, 133
    See also Equality of Jesus with God
Unjust judge, parable of — 59
Unleavened Bread, feast of — *See* Passover
Unprofitable servant, parable of — 78ff
Upstairs room — *See* Cenacle

— V —

Victory — 131
Vine and branches — 80ff
Vinedressers, parable of — 118ff
Virgin Mary — *See* Mary, Mother of Jesus
Visitation — 18
Voice of good shepherd — 95ff, 110
    See also Father, voice of

— W —

Walking on water — 87ff

Washing of apostles' feet —
122ff

Water changed into wine —
37ff
  Living water — 129

Way, Jesus as — 127
  See also Life; Truth
Wedding at Cana — 37ff

Wedding guests, parable of
  bridegroom and — 45ff
Weeds (tares), parable of —
  66
Wine, water changed into
  — 37ff

  Of Good Samaritan —
    54
  At Last Supper — 125
  At Calvary — 147, 151
Wisdom of Jesus — 27
  See also Prophet, Jesus
    as

Wise Men — 25ff

Witnesses to Jesus — 74ff,
  98, 128
    False — 141
    See also Ambassadors
Wolf — 95
Wolf pack — 75
Woman of Destiny — 37,
  149
Women of Jerusalem — 147
Worry — 27, 76, 126
Worship — See Prayer;
  Prayer of Jesus

— Y —

Yeast, parable of — 67

— Z —

Zachary — 13ff, 18
Zebedee — 42, 74, 162
  See also Salome Zebe-
    dee